"This valuable and lucidly written book is a beautiful integration, theoretically and practically, that shows how schema therapy can be enriched by concepts and practices from coherence therapy to identify, strategically target, and permanently update specific beliefs and predictions encoded in the range of early maladaptive schema systems. It is a wonderful resource for promoting schema healing."

David Edwards, *emeritus professor at Rhodes University in South Africa, clinical psychologist (South Africa and UK), ISST-certified trainer, and former ISST president*

"The work of Cousineau and Côté has been an inspiration for me, and I believe that schema therapy and its development gain a lot by this book. I therefore recommend it with great pleasure!"

Remco van der Wijngaart, *chair of the Dutch Society of Schema Therapy (VSt) and director/owner of the Dutch Institute for Schema Therapy*

"This masterful book by Cousineau and Côté is a tremendous service, not only to schema therapy and its worldwide practitioners, but also to the psychotherapy field as a whole, because it shows how to retool and maximize the effectiveness of a well-established therapy system with our 21st-century knowledge of memory reconsolidation as the brain's core process of liberating, transformational change."

Bruce Ecker, *LMFT, co-founder of coherence therapy, co-director of the Coherence Psychology Institute, and co-author of* Unlocking the Emotional Brain

"Cousineau and Côté present a thoughtful roadmap for aligning the strengths of schema therapy with a precise understanding of what the brain needs to truly unlearn entrenched predictive models. This book is a generous and valuable contribution to the global community of therapists."

Tori Olds, PhD, *co-founder of Deep Eddy Psychotherapy, one of the largest therapy and training centers in Texas, USA*

SCHEMA THERAPY FOR MEMORY RECONSOLIDATION AND TRANSFORMATIONAL CHANGE

Schema Therapy for Memory Reconsolidation and Transformational Change offers psychotherapists a model for clearly and coherently conceptualizing human complexity in a transparent, accessible form.

The book explores the pivotal concept of schemas, which are the emotional memories built up through our life experiences that largely determine our view of the world and the way we react and adapt to it. Schema therapy focuses on certain early schemas that have become maladaptive. It has always done so with openness, integrating techniques from a variety of psychotherapeutic orientations.

The book presents schemas in their predictive function and looks at the possibility of updating these predictions based on advances in neuroscience that clarify the conditions necessary for therapeutic reconsolidation of memory.

Pierre Cousineau is a psychologist in private practice in Montréal. He practices, teaches, and writes about schema therapy, supervises psychotherapists, and integrates therapeutic memory reconsolidation into his approach.

Sophie Côté is a psychologist in private practice in Québec. She is interested in the impact of psychotherapy on the brain and is an expert in therapeutic memory reconsolidation in humans and animals. She practices, teaches, and writes about coherence therapy and supervises psychotherapists.

SCHEMA THERAPY FOR MEMORY RECONSOLIDATION AND TRANSFORMATIONAL CHANGE

Pierre Cousineau and Sophie Côté

Routledge
Taylor & Francis Group
NEW YORK AND LONDON

Designed cover image: "Renaissance" by Danielle Belotte.
Image used with permission of the artist

First English edition published 2026
by Routledge
605 Third Avenue, New York, NY 10158

and by Routledge
4 Park Square, Milton Park, Abingdon, Oxon OX14 4RN

Routledge is an imprint of the Taylor & Francis Group, an informa business

First French edition published by Dunod 2023

Originally published in France as:
Pratiquer la thérapie des schémas. Transformer les modèles prédictifs avec la reconsolidation de la mémoire by Pierre COUSINEAU and Sophie CÔTÉ.

ISBN: 9781041043799 (hbk)
ISBN: 9781041043782 (pbk)
ISBN: 9781003628125 (ebk)

DOI: 10.4324/9781003628125

Typeset in Galliard
by Newgen Publishing UK

Contents

Figures

The Purpose of This Book

Schema Therapy (ST) offers an enlightening conceptualization of the different facets of human experience in an accessible language while providing an operational definition of the aims of therapy. Its vocabulary is simple without being simplistic; what's more, its ease of use means that we can openly share with patients our understanding of how they function and what is happening in the therapeutic process. Since Jeffrey Young's first publication (1990) on early maladaptive schemas (EMS), this approach has steadily gained in importance. It is now practiced in many countries around the world.

When it comes to EMS, one question regularly pops up: Is it possible to substantially transform these schemas, even totally annul and rewrite them, or, instead, should we aim to create strategies for managing them? If there is one universally shared human experience, it is the difficulty of changing our patterns, whether in our thoughts, emotions, or behaviors. Think of a "bad" habit you would like to change; change is most often associated with a lot of willpower, effort … and a high risk of relapse. Schemas, as we will remind you in this book, have a long-standing reputation for being hard-wired … and hard to change.

We will also review in this book how schemas are learnings stored in memory. Dealing with the reactivation of these memories is a significant therapeutic objective in itself, but working with them in a way that would fundamentally transform them has long been the dream of most psychotherapists. The jealous person who seeks your help will be happy to learn how to better control their impulsive tendencies when their abandonment anxiety is triggered (Abandonment schema) but would certainly prefer to simply not experience the anxiety in the first place and therefore not have to resort to multiple mental and behavioral strategies to keep regulating it. For this second option to become reality, we need access to tools that can radically transform memory. We must ask specifically: What interventions on memory can transform it and consequently transform schemas? It was through our shared interest in this question that Sophie Côté and I began collaborating. The work of Bruce Ecker and his colleagues on the therapeutic reconsolidation of memory has led us to the answers we were looking for. As a direct application of neuroscience research findings, Ecker and colleagues (2012, 2024) defined the therapeutic reconsolidation process (TRP) as an atheoretic, technique-independent map of methodology for consistently inducing memory reconsolidation to produce transformational therapeutic change. Our invaluable connection with these clinicians combined with our own practical and reflective approach led us to write our first book, *La reconsolidation thérapeutique de la mémoire*,[1] published by Dunod in 2022. Building on this experience, we came up with the idea for the present book.[2]

And what exactly is that idea? To integrate the power of memory reconsolidation with the effectiveness and accessibility of ST. Schema Therapy offers therapists a model that provides a clear, coherent conceptualization of human complexity in a transparent, accessible form. It is a wonderful map for navigating the dense forest of human experience. Often, simply through mentalization,[3] the first therapeutic impact is felt by the patient. All their reactions at last make sense: My way of being is not abnormal, I'm not crazy. I can even understand why I have all these reactions and why I needed to develop all these strategies. But the next therapeutic challenge is, as we mentioned earlier, to manage or modify the schemas. ST already offers several avenues for achieving either of these goals. However, Sophie and I are convinced that the therapeutic reconsolidation process (TRP) of memory is a royal road to targeted modification of schemas through direct intervention on their memory traces. To continue with the analogy of the forest, identifying a schema leads us to the foot of a tree (the schema), which is already a huge advantage over wandering around the forest without landmarks. But once we've reached the foot of the tree, the TRP requires us to locate the branch that corresponds to the exact way the schema is constituted for the individual patient we are working with, the schema's specific memory trace in this person. For example, an Abandonment schema may be based on very different learning experiences from one person to another, involving a specific interaction between external and internal threats and resources, giving rise to an infinite number of nuances. As we explained in our previous book, the experiential shift necessary for memory reconsolidation requires a very specific experience (a **living** knowledge that is fundamentally incompatible with the schema's model of reality), the discovery of which requires the precise identification of the branch (perhaps even the leaves) on which the target memory rests. All these concepts are, of course, explained in greater detail in this book.

Two basic and essential concepts are used when working with ST, schema modes and schemas (EMS), and both are fundamentally linked to basic psychological needs ("core emotional needs"). These concepts were first defined in Young's textbook (Young et al., 2003); there were then 18 EMS and 10 schema modes. Since then, there have been several proposals for ramifications to the model. For example, we find 23 schema modes in a recent publication by several well-known schema therapists (Brockman et al., 2023).

Our aim in this book is not to present all the issues raised in the ST world. For that, several publications already exist (Behary, 2021; Behary et al., 2023; Brockman et al., 2023; Edwards, 2022; Farrell & Shaw, 2012; Farrell et al., 2014; Loose et al., 2020; Roediger et al., 2018; Simpson, 2020; van der Wijngaart, 2021). It is more about proposing the integration of our expertise in therapeutic memory reconsolidation to schema interventions. We will therefore use as a basis the 18 schemas and ten schema modes as presented originally by Young et al. (2003).[4,5]

As will be seen later in this book, schemas form a specific category of memory, which makes predictions from what it recognizes, determining at the same time which adaptive response to produce to avoid suffering assessed as intolerable. This conception is in line with an important neuropsychological movement that emphasizes the pivotal role of the brain's predictive functions (Barrett, 2018; Clark, 2023; Hohwy, 2013; Seth, 2021; Solms, 2021). In Coherence Therapy (Ecker et al., 2012, 2024; Côté & Cousineau, 2022), the intervention model is based directly on the TRP, and the patients' problems are understood as perfectly coherent because patients are considered to be tolerating what is perceived as a lesser suffering to avoid a worse suffering. We will see how well this conceptual framework can be applied to ST concepts like schema maintenance, explicitly opening the door to radical schema transformation.

In our book on memory reconsolidation (Côté & Cousineau, 2022), we used two important templates: the Resources/Threats Matrix illustrating the perceptual process behind schemas developed by Sophie Côté, and the Schema Map developed by both authors. We will be using these templates to illustrate how the TRP can be integrated with ST. This integration we are proposing will simply constitute a new way of organizing the presentation of schemas without substantially altering the nature of the concepts used in ST.

Notes

1 *Therapeutic Memory Reconsolidation: Transforming Emotional Schemas with Coherence Therapy*
2 First published in French (Cousineau & Côté, 2023)
3 Mentalization is a therapeutic technique which consists of explicitly describing to ourselves our various emotional experiences (Fonagy et al., 2002). For example, the fear that you'll abandon me drives me to check the messages on your phone. In ST, we would say the reactivation of my Abandonment schema leads me to use a counterattacking (overcompensating) strategy, seeking to control the threat.
4 The position adopted by Wendy Behary, Joan Farrell, and Jeffrey Young in a workshop at the 2024 ISST World Conference in Warsaw has reinforced the choice we made.
5 For those already familiar with ST: It should be noted that the many modes added later can easily be understood as being sub-modes to those of the original model, for example, ways of describing more specifically the Protector–Avoidance mode (Detached Protector, Detached Self-Soother, etc.) or Overcompensator mode (Self-Aggrandizer, Perfectionistic Overcontroller, Bully and Attack, etc.). Presenting the original model will be sufficient to enable understanding of how to integrate the model into the principles underlying the TRP and will facilitate understanding of the model itself.

Part I

Schema Therapy and Our Adaptive Learning Systems

Chapter 1
Schemas Illuminated by Neuroscience

I remember when Erika arrived for her weekly session with me, Sophie Côté (SC). She had just had a terrible fight with her partner minutes before coming online. She was on the verge of tears, still shaking from their interaction, and blaming herself for having frozen during the argument like a terrified little girl. Right away, I recognized she was overwhelmed with anxiety, and I could feel that her distress also activated a compassionate and caring response from me; I wanted to make her feel safe and secure in our therapeutic space. Let's look at my case example from a constructivist perspective, which is the epistemological approach of this book.

According to this perspective, reality, as we perceive it, react to it, and describe it, is understood as an elaboration of our brain, whose complexity has enabled the emergence of our intricate mental life with all its representations, images, and concepts (Barrett, 2018; Clark, 2023; Damasio, 2021; Seth, 2021; Solms, 2021). The stimuli from the outside world,[1] like Erika's distress signals or her partner's emotional signals during the argument, first passed through Erika's and my exteroceptive and interoceptive senses. The signals were then filtered through several internal structures that constructed our perceptions of what was going on inside and outside ourselves, creating the subjective experiences I described from the beginning of our session together.

Although they disagree on the role played by what we will later refer to as phylogenetic memory, Lisa Barrett (2018) and Mark Solms (2021) agree that our relationships to reality are mediated by constructs; Barrett goes so far as to call them everyday hallucinations, and Seth (2021), for his part, uses the expression "controlled hallucinations." These constructs

DOI: 10.4324/9781003628125-2

are referred to in a variety of ways, such as mental models, concepts, and schemas.

This book will deal specifically with the eighteen early maladaptive schemas identified by Young in his classic work published in 2003 (Young et al., 2003). These schemas constitute a subcategory of the numerous schemas a person could construct.

Let's start by looking at what processes support the creation of schemas, what type of memory they correspond to, and what their function is.

Panksepp's Basic Emotional Systems: Phylogenetic Memory

To understand where schemas come from, let's start from the beginning: our phylogenetic memory (DNA). Even if our mental activity[2] is not limited to the brain, there is still a strong consensus in the scientific community that the brain is its essential foundation. According to Panksepp (Panksepp, 1998; Panksepp & Biven, 2012), there are innate affective systems in humans (as well as in many animals) that serve as the basis for our multiple emotional experiences, including those experienced by Erika and SC during their session. These systems have retained the mechanisms that favored the adaptive evolution of our species. For example, Erika could not just decide to stop experiencing fear or lust in her relationship, no more than her partner could simply decide to stop experiencing rage; we all have to find ways of living with these affective systems. Sometimes the selected solution is dissociation from them, but even this can only be done at some cost to our energy budget.[3] Referring to Panksepp's "instinctual" emotional systems, Solms (2021) uses terminology that resonates with our idea of highlighting the distinction between phylogenetic memory and memory of experience:

> [O]ur reflexes and instincts provide rough-and-ready tools for survival and reproductive success, but they cannot possibly equip us adequately for the multiplicity of unpredicted situations and environments that we find ourselves in. We, therefore, need to adaptively supplement the innate responses through learning from experience.[...]
>
> The instinctual programs that undergird actions in humans are typically so conditioned through learning that they are no longer

> recognizable as 'instinctual.' Yet instincts and reflexes are always there in the background.
>
> (pp. 104–105)

Panksepp has identified seven fundamental emotional systems, each of which he associates with a primary process involving "ancestral memories." These systems are located in the primitive parts of the brain (midbrain, limbic system nuclei, etc.). These primary affective systems are at the root of all our emotional reactions—however sophisticated these reactions may be—in much the same way as blue, red, and yellow are at the root of the whole palette of colors in a painting.

Let's take a brief look at these seven basic emotional systems and illustrate them using Erika's therapy session.

Seeking. The SEEKING[4] system is considered our default system because it tends to occupy our emotional space when nothing urgent or important is mobilizing other systems. It also provides the other systems with the information they need to update their functions.

When a very young child's basic needs (food, security, affection, sleep, etc.) are met, they exercise their curiosity and explore and manipulate objects in the environment. Most of the time, this is done with pleasure, even enthusiasm.

The SEEKING system encourages us to be curious, to try to understand how the world works, and to question how human beings function. As a result, writing this book is a highly enjoyable activity for us, and we are naturally inclined to cogitate on the various ways in which we could improve its content. This constant and very active research provides us with subjective nourishment.

But the SEEKING system also plays a role in avoidance or control of what seems unpleasant. In this way, it pushes us to develop resources to protect ourselves or eliminate what could become threatening or unpleasant. As she was describing her fight with her partner, Erika was frantically exploring several ways in which she could have triggered his anger in the hope of being able to make amends and avoid this situation happening again in the future.

Interestingly, Solms (2021) points out that when combined with the LUST system discussed later, the SEEKING system becomes, in short, the equivalent of what Freud meant by libido—that desire which makes us sensitive to certain contexts, certain signals, and which propels us forward to achieve satisfaction of needs and desires.[5]

In its spontaneous version, the SEEKING system arouses curiosity, interest, and enthusiasm. Imagine a young child having fun opening and closing drawers, manipulating pots and pans, and so forth. Later in life, this child, who has become an adult with access to symbolic tools, may play with abstract mathematical concepts in the same way they used to play with pots and pans! The SEEKING system creates its own reinforcements, such as the simple pleasure of knowing and learning (which we hope you are experiencing as you read this book). This is the dopaminergic system, dopamine being a neurohormone that has become part of the vernacular.

Fear. As soon as she heard the tension in her partner's voice, Erika knew an escalation would happen, and she felt her stomach clench. Our survival depends on us having an effective alarm system that alerts us immediately when our safety is threatened. The function of the FEAR system is to respond to this imperative. It mobilizes the organism to move away from a threat (injury, death, intimidation, etc.). Initially dedicated to preserving our biological survival, FEAR has extended to our capacity for symbolic construction; this explains why the apprehension of being ridiculed can terrorize us just as much as that of being punched in the face. Erika's FEAR system alerted her in anticipation of her husband's tendency to become angry during an argument, even though she did not perceive that her physical integrity was at risk.

The FEAR system is part of what Panksepp calls the primary process of brain function, with the amygdala and regions of the midbrain (PAG) playing a fundamental role. This is true of all the primary affective systems identified by Panksepp. One of us (PC) has a striking example from personal experience illustrating the function of this system. During his encounter with a two-meter-long Indian cobra in Nepal in 2001, his FEAR system was mobilized in a split second even though he had never had such a close experience with a snake before (in this case, learning via experience would have been fatal), his avoidance reaction keeping him alive. And, through association, a simple branch encountered later on a hiking trail may, for a few brief seconds, trigger the prediction of an imminent threat.

Panic/Grief. In everyday language, and even among many professionals, the PANIC/GRIEF system is often confused with the FEAR system. However, they are two different systems (Panksepp & Biven, 2012; Solms, 2021). Fear is triggered when we predict a direct threat to our safety (physical, emotional, or psychological), whereas panic is linked to our attachment system. It is triggered when there is estrangement from or loss of the attachment figure (initially, the mother or any person occupying the mothering role). Think of a very young child who, having ventured into the aisles of a store (SEEKING system), suddenly realizes they can no longer see their mother. Or watch a wildlife report in which you hear the shrill cries of young animals whose mothers have wandered off.

The terrible discomfort experienced when the PANIC/GRIEF system is triggered fosters the strength of the attachment bonds essential to a young child's survival. It is not a good idea to go too far away from your source of security, given the risk of experiencing great suffering. We will see later that the parent's CARE system is the perfect complement to this need for secure proximity.

Erika's PANIC system was definitely online during our session as she described how her partner had stormed out of the house, which usually meant that he would take several hours to calm down and refuse to answer his phone or reply to her messages. At that moment, she suffered acutely from the rupture of their bond and, although she knew their relationship was not over, she felt the distance between them.

Maturity will favor a form of mutation from panic to sadness. A person's type of response to a relational loss is an indication of how well that person's PANIC/GRIEF emotional system is integrated into the higher cortical networks. Some adults still react to this type of loss with panic responses that can lead to despair, which is Erika's case, while others experience sadness instead. Sadness, although painful, does not lead to the same level of suffering as panic.

Rage. When things do not go as planned, when an obstacle prevents us from meeting our needs, when what is happening upsets us, and we want the situation to change to be in line with our intentions, the RAGE system is mobilized. At the beginning of human life, this system expresses itself brutally; a child may bite, hit, or kick if they consider themselves wronged by another child (unfortunately, some adults remain at this stage). Babies will also express their discomfort through this system. When they are cold, hungry, in pain, or uncomfortable in a wet diaper, they will express their rage, indicating that the situation does not suit them and that things must change. The baby does not express this intention specifically, but the message is received by others, loud and clear, nonetheless.

The RAGE system is the basis of our ability to defend ourselves. As we will see later on, it is the foundation of Angry Child mode, an internal resource which, when wisely used, enables us to stop tolerating situations where our physical or psychological integrity is not being respected.

When properly socialized (through secondary and tertiary brain function processes, which will be covered in the next section), RAGE becomes what we call anger. When used judiciously, anger is a fundamental internal resource in human adaptation. It provides the energy we need to secure and defend our place in the world. Fortunately for Erika, her socialized RAGE system eventually came online during our session when she told her partner in an imagery exercise:

"I didn't like what you did, and I won't tolerate it anymore," and "I didn't like what you said, and I won't accept you talking to me like that anymore."

She expressed that something bothered her and that it must change. Erika's healthy assertiveness was made possible by the motivational energy received from the RAGE system.

Since Schema Therapy (ST) is concerned with people's basic needs and how they express them, paying attention to anger is seen as a therapeutic goal to help the person adapt effectively to their environment. Thanks to our neocortex, we can assert ourselves in a socially appropriate way by choosing how to express our anger judiciously. For example, we may recognize that we are feeling angry, but if we are in the presence of an explosive person prone to physical violence, we may choose to postpone our assertion to another time, knowing that the consequences of expressing ourselves right away could be disastrous. We are, therefore, capable of recognizing the activation of anger within our body and choosing whether to express it. For this to happen, our RAGE system must be socialized; people who have not had the necessary experiences for socialization of rage will react, even in adulthood, as a young child would. When a situation does not suit them, they flatly refuse to accept it. Think of a man whose spouse tells him she no longer loves him and wants to leave him and whose RAGE system has not been socialized. He could then forbid her to leave him, assault her, or even kill her. This is a tragic example of what an unsocialized RAGE system can do. Fortunately for Erika, her partner's RAGE system was socialized enough for him to limit his behavior to raising his voice and slamming the front door on his way out.

- The FEAR, PANIC/GRIEF, and RAGE systems manifest themselves in contexts of danger and threat. They are fundamental to our survival (staying inside a burning house is not a good idea), but most often unpleasant to experience—unless they are experienced in situations that we choose and can control, such as a rollercoaster ride. In this type of context, the SEEKING system is often also along for the ride.
- In contrast, the following three fundamental emotional systems are quite pleasant to experience. In a way similar to the spontaneous version of the SEEKING system, they correspond to subjective states that we enjoy and seek to maintain and repeat. But our survival and adaptation as individuals and as a species are linked to these next systems in the same way as they are to the three previous ones.

Lust. This system is associated with sexual motivation and reproductive behavior. According to Panksepp, the LUST system is driven by hormonal influences, particularly those related to sex hormones like testosterone and estrogen. As with all the other primary emotional systems, the manifestation of the LUST system requires maturation and socialization. It is not acceptable to impose our sexual desire on another person (this would be sexual aggression). Therefore, the primary system needs to be integrated into our learning processes so that sexual intimacy can take place within a framework of mutual consent.

Care. A human baby cannot survive on its own. Reproduction of the species, therefore, requires something other than sexuality; the child needs care until it becomes autonomous. But this cannot be left to chance or goodwill. The evolution of the human species (as well as that of many animals) has therefore led to the creation of another phylogenetic memory, the CARE system, which fulfils this purpose. For example, for most of us, what could be more irresistible than a child's smile? Even when we know the smile is caused by a reflex mechanism, it doesn't change much; it still melts our hearts!

The CARE and PANIC/GRIEF systems constantly interact in the attachment dynamic. For example, let's remember our toddler we imagined earlier, who ventured into another aisle at the supermarket. If the child got separated from the parent, the child would likely start crying in distress (PANIC). Hearing the cries, the parent would realize the toddler has left their side and feel the urge to find the child immediately and then soothe the child's distress with hugs and by humming softly (CARE). The child, feeling the parent's warm embrace and soothing voice, would calm down and feel secure again (CARE), which in return would soothe the parent.

This kind of interaction is also part of the therapeutic relationship: In answer to Erika's distress, the therapist felt a genuine urge to take care of her and provide a safe place where she could settle down, be helped, be seen, and so forth. And when in touch with her therapist's compassion and attention to her needs, Erika responded accordingly.

Play. The PLAY system is another basic emotional system that does not spontaneously spring to mind for most of us. Yet Panksepp believes it serves a very important role in socialization and development of self-control.

Anyone who works with children will have noticed that they tend to tug at each other, to squabble—most often in laughter and fun. It is not uncommon for this pleasure to eventually turn to tears for one of the protagonists, which in no way prevents the ritualized fight from being resumed at another time. This game is known as "rough-and-tumble." Its social virtue, according to Panksepp, is to enable the child to experience the positions of domination and submission. Play then requires an alternation of these positions with at least a 60-40 rule of reciprocity (Solms, 2021); without this distribution, there is no more play, but the domination of one child over another. When the level of reciprocity is appropriate, both children have the opportunity to learn the notion of limits in interaction (self-control).

What's more, at its best, play requires the other person to agree to play with you. This means you have to take their feelings into account.

Pierre Cousineau (PC), raised in Québec in the fifties, likes to relate the following anecdote during training sessions. In those days, most mothers stayed at home, overburdened by the many domestic tasks required in the daily life of large families. Often, our mother would open the door in the morning and tell us to go out and play and not come home until lunchtime. The same thing happened in the afternoon. In those days, children didn't go to nursery or day-care—services that simply did not exist. So, this "wild horde" of children was left to its own devices. With no educators or monitors, we had to decide for ourselves which games to play. Back then, in Montréal, hockey-related games or what we used to call "Cowboys and Indians"[6] were the favorites. But, left to ourselves, we had to figure out the rules of the game (i.e., how to decide which of the belligerents had been killed). Although this was not always done in perfect harmony (bullies aren't new to the twenty-first century), we managed pretty well most of the time. This type of play was an opportunity for us to learn about the self-managed balance between competition and cooperation. This is one of the enormous contributions of the PLAY system.

Play can be derailed into other systems: aggression, fear, and sexual play. This is why Panksepp recommends adult supervision that is not too interventionist in children's play and that does not inhibit a child's fundamental need to play spontaneously, including the famous "rough-and-tumble" that is both necessary and difficult to tolerate for many contemporary parents, schools, and day-care systems!

The Memory of Personal Experience

We have just summarized Panksepp's categorization of primary affective systems, which are not the result of our individual experience but rather that of our species. Before moving on to the memory of experience, we want to make one final comment about what we have called phylogenetic memory. We observe a connection with Panksepp's basic emotional systems and temperament. Young et al. (2003) emphasizes the role of temperament in the creation of schemas:

> Factors other than early childhood environment also play major roles in the development of schemas. The child's emotional temperament is especially important. As most parents soon realize, each child has a unique and distinct "personality" or temperament from birth. Some children are more irritable, some are more shy, some are more aggressive.
>
> (p. 11)

We suggest that the relative strength of each fundamental emotional system could reflect an individual's temperament.

But, as we will soon see, most of our psychotherapy interventions are aimed at what Panksepp categorizes as secondary and tertiary processes. Erika did not come to therapy to change her primary processes, even if several of them were involved in her distressing argument with her partner. It is simply not possible to erase our DNA. This is fortunate because these systems are fundamental to our survival. Imagine a form of therapy that could remove fear from military personnel, who then found themselves deployed to a war zone; it wouldn't do them any favors!

So why do people come to therapy? Because some of the things they have learned make it so that their emotional systems generate significant suffering instead of working in their favor. Psychotherapy can change learning based on experience because what has been learned can be managed differently and even unlearned if the therapeutic reconsolidation process is used appropriately. Primary affective systems, used judiciously in therapy, are often indispensable allies in our work on learning that has become dysfunctional. Think of a person who was abused as a child and whose RAGE system is socialized through therapy into a healthy sense of anger (by leveraging secondary and tertiary systems). This will also serve to transform the person's construct of powerlessness in the face of current abusive situations. Let's now take a closer look at those secondary and tertiary systems.

Panksepp's Secondary Processes. This secondary level is extremely important because it is here that schemas are created. For example, when we have a need (felt in our primary systems), the memory of our experiences will help us predict what will happen when we express this need. Will there be a response or not? Will the expression of my need activate my parent's CARE system or their RAGE system? Primary affective systems are in constant interaction with the world, and this is what will determine our predictions about our relationships as well as our environment. This is where things get complex, because the range of answers to our needs is so vast. When the gap between needs and responses becomes too wide, and our predictions have become rigid, the apprehended suffering becomes too great, and the solutions, in the absence of appropriate resources, are often too rudimentary. We then find ourselves in the domain of early maladaptive schemas, as described by Young.

Panksepp (Panksepp & Biven, 2012) locates secondary processes in the brain's basal ganglia, including the amygdala, nucleus accumbens, and bed nucleus of the stria terminalis. It is important to understand that we are still talking about systems that are in subcortical areas of the brain and, therefore, involved in implicit information processing. These structures form the substratum of our automatic habits, including the unwanted ones that most often motivate people to consult a therapist. It is to these habits that people are referring when they say, "I can't help it."

Learning takes place by creating associations, according to Hebb's famous principle[7] (Hebb, 2009). For example, when we react to a tree branch lying across a path as if it were an Indian cobra (generalization of a shape associated with danger), or Proust's famous madeleines from *À la recherche du temps perdu*,[8] which, offered with tea by his mother, reminded him of those he was served at his aunt Léonie's in Combray, which then reminded him of multiple images from that period of his childhood.[9] An association reminds us, implicitly or explicitly, that this comes with that. One of us (PC) also recounts in training sessions the unpleasant sensation he experienced as an adult upon returning to his childhood elementary school. He experienced the unpleasant sensation before the explicit memory associated with it resurfaced (sticking his tongue on the schoolyard's frozen metal fence in winter, a far less poetic example than Proust's madeleines!). Again, the unpleasant sensation in no way required the episodic memory to manifest itself.

These associations are created through well-known processes such as respondent conditioning, operant conditioning, mimicry, and generalization. But the principle is always the same: **this comes with that**, which will form the source of our predictions about ourselves, others, and the world. And, at the secondary level, they are mostly implicit. Siegel (2012) describes this type of memory very well with expressions like "implicit knowing," "implicit memory," and "implicit mental processes." An implicit memory comes with the subjective impression that its origin cannot be located in time; we have no explicit recollection of having learned it. That is why it is most often attributed to a personal characteristic rather than learning: "I'm made like that; that's just the way I am." Therefore, it is not surprising that this is where we locate the early maladaptive schemas identified by Young. Here is what Siegel (2012) writes about implicit memory:

> Involves parts of the brain that do not require conscious, focal attention during encoding or retrieval. Perceptions, emotions, bodily sensations, and behavioral response patterns are all examples of implicit layers of processing. Mental models (schema or generalizations of repeated experiences) and priming (getting ready to respond) are basic components. Implicit memory, in its nonintegrated form, lacks a sense that something is being recalled from the past.
>
> (pp. 340–341)

We find it useful to distinguish between two main types of learning, statistical learning and rapid learning, the latter often found in contexts of trauma or at least very intense emotional reactions.

Statistical learning is the most common; it involves extracting characteristics that are common to different things or situations. For example, I learn that when my father's voice gets deep, it is not the right time to ask him for something, or that when I need to tell someone what happened at school, no one will express any caring—several repeated interpersonal interactions lead to the creation of such associations. Statistical learning is responsible for much of our learning: sensorimotor, language, affective, symbols, and so on. Barrett (2018) describes this type of learning very well:

> Babies use statistical learning to make predictions about the world, guiding their actions. Like little statisticians, they form hypotheses, assess probabilities based on their knowledge, integrate new evidence from the environment, and perform tests. [...] Infants are not merely reactive to the world. Even from a very young age, they actively estimate probabilities.
>
> (pp. 95–96)

As for rapid learning, this is often based on a single event ("one-trial-learning") or at least happens in a very short time. Trauma-causing situations are the most obvious examples. Being the victim of an armed robbery, a physical or sexual assault, or a serious car accident are all relevant examples, although, as we will see later, the resources available to us will have an impact on how we deal with these situations; they may or may not result in post-traumatic stress.

To fully understand the nature of schemas, another major paradigm needs to be introduced, namely that of the schema's fundamental function: prediction. Indeed, memory of experience serves to prepare us for what lies ahead by allowing us to manage our energy budget in the most optimal way possible. Not having to re-evaluate every situation as if it were completely new represents an immense advantage. If we had to do so, we would require a gigantic amount of brain energy to function, which would create a permanent imbalance in the distribution of our somatic energy.

The predictive function of schemas has been amply explained in our first book on the therapeutic memory reconsolidation process (Côté & Cousineau, 2022), but let's review the main points here.

- Predictions are at the root of how the brain works—the "remembered present" means the brain is constantly on the lookout for what is coming next by **recognizing** what it is interacting with.
- These predictions are based on similar past experiences, enabling the brain to make sense of the inner (interoceptive) and outer (sensorimotor) world.
- Again, based on our previous experiences, the brain determines **what the world looks like**, **what is going to happen**, and **what the best response to that is**.
- This prediction takes the form of a **simulation of what is to come** and **what can be done about it**.
- So, the brain does not simply react to the world, it predicts and constructs experience. In this way, **perception and memory are inseparable**.

Here is an example of what this might look like in real life. After their fight, Erika sends an email to her partner to make amends. Two hours later, she still has not received a reply. The prediction activated in Erika's brain is that her partner is punishing her with the silent treatment (what is recognized) and that he is not replying because he is angry (what will happen). For Erika, this is a simulation of some of her childhood situations where a parent regularly got angry with her and accused her of being selfish (what it looks like). Erika rereads her e-mail, examining it from every possible angle to identify what might have offended her partner; she writes another e-mail to try to mitigate her apprehended mistake (perceived best response).

This leads us to a fundamental qualitative characteristic of secondary processes: what is experienced through them seems true; it is a world we construct for ourselves—at the moment we do so, we do not imagine there could be any other reality. This is what we call an **emotional truth**.

The concept of emotional truth serves to explain the limitations of certain interventions such as cognitive restructuring; for example, it is virtually impossible to convince Erika, who suffers from imposter syndrome, that she is worthy using rational arguments—chances are she will say something like, "Yes, I understand, but it doesn't change how I feel."

People consult a therapist because their learning has led them to experience unpleasant affects, of course, but above all, because their ways of avoiding these unpleasant affects end up causing problems for them. In Acceptance and Commitment Therapy (ACT), for example, the underlying process behind all psychological problems is considered to be experiential avoidance. Psychodynamic approaches argue that we avoid contact with issues that create inordinate amounts of anxiety for us. The threat signals that something unpleasant will happen and that we'd better try avoiding it. But why is one person afraid of flying while another anticipates it with excitement? Why is the same situation a threat to one person and not to another? It is all based on predictions. If a person predicts that taking a plane will be like taking a walk, the perception of threat will be low. On the other hand, if a person associates flying with a life-threatening activity, the perceived threat will be high.

To further answer this question, one of us (SC) has developed a matrix illustrating the perception process that is behind schemas based on the synergy between resource and threat perception (see Figure 1.1).

This matrix emphasizes that the determination of what constitutes a threat depends on the interplay between predictions about the intensity of a threat (a rabid dog versus a headache) and predictions about the resources available to us (a bike to use as a shield against a rabid dog, knowledge of self-defense techniques, knowledge of first aid, possession of painkillers). Also, as you can see in Figure 1.1, the origin of a threat or resource can be external or internal. For human beings, an example of an excellent external resource is an emotional connection with another human being (Coan et al., 2006; Coan & Sbarra, 2015). And, as we will see later on, the ability to function from a Healthy Adult mode is an example of an optimal internal resource.

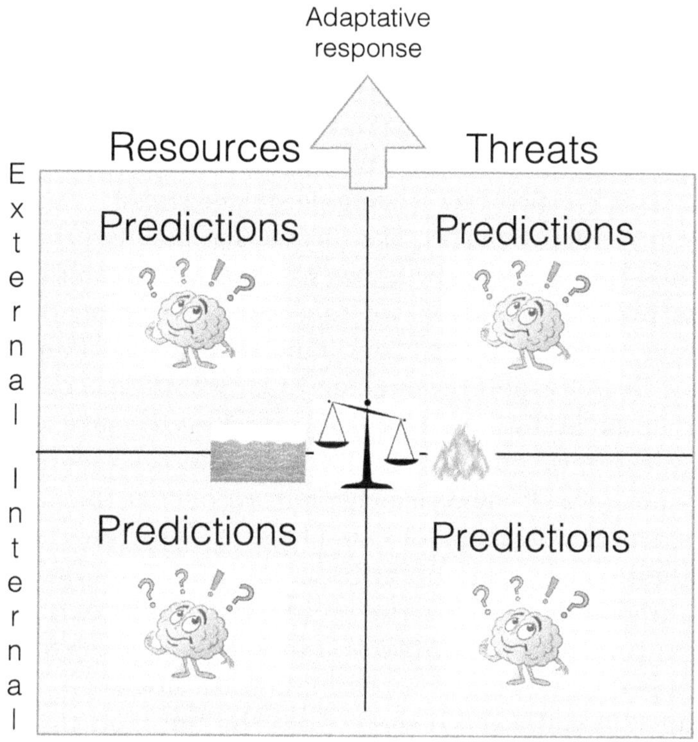

Figure 1.1 *Resources/Threats Matrix here*

Let's now flesh out the Resources/Threats Matrix a bit and see if it stirs up some experiential memories for you as therapists.

Threats come either from the outside (an external prediction) or from within (an internal prediction). In human beings, the threat is very often mixed. Consider the case of a client who was terrified of upsetting others because she had been physically abused by her mother. Feeling angry was perceived as—and therefore predicted to be—dangerous, because anger, if heeded and expressed, would provoke her mother's violent behavior, putting the client in danger. The threat is thus mixed: through statistical learning, the construct of "feeling anger is dangerous" is created; anger thus becomes perceived as an internal threat since it puts her in danger of triggering an external threat (her mother's violent reactions, generalized to anyone she might upset).

One of the worst perceived threats is that of being left alone (lack of a fundamental external resource and pain from the PANIC/GRIEF system). This makes perfect sense when it comes to children: a child left completely alone will die, as they will be without resources not only to ensure sustenance but also to defend against external threats. The "silent treatment" is another way in which a child can be left alone, as in the case of Erika, who, when she upset her mother, the latter would stop speaking to her for days on end. Here again, the threat is mixed: my dissatisfaction, if expressed, will cause me to be isolated from my external resources for several days, creating excruciating personal distress.

We see here that resources, like threats, can be internal or external. When a child feels overwhelmed, they will look for an external resource. The most positive prediction we can have concerning our external resources as children is that our emotional connection with our attachment figures is good enough and that we will be comforted and assisted if we are in distress. If we have experienced a sufficiently secure attachment bond, we can then develop good internal resources.

Predictions take all these elements into account at the same time. If Erika experiences a breakup, for example, she will perceive the extent of the threat not only in terms of the break-up and the unpleasant internal reaction it triggers but also in terms of the internal and external resources available to cope with it. If Erika is convinced that she has missed her only chance of ever being in a relationship because she is a mediocre person, she will suffer much more from the break-up than someone convinced that other relationships are still possible. The same threat (for example, an uncomfortable medical examination) will be perceived as less important if external and internal resources are available to deal with it. That is why we have added a pan balance and the symbols of fire and water to our figure. If resources are almost non-existent, the fire will grow and grow because nothing can stop it. On the other hand, if we have resources, we can extinguish the fire, or at least fight it, by having, for example, self-compassion for ourselves in a difficult moment. At one end of this continuum, we see trauma, which is when the threat takes up all the space, and there are no resources available to modulate it. The person experiences a feeling of powerlessness: the threat is too great, there's nothing I can do about it, and it's going to completely overwhelm me, annihilate me.

The adaptive response is coherent with this Resources/Threats Matrix. For example, if my predictions indicate that I will be surrounded by support if I express my distress, my adaptive response will be to reach out to people when I am suffering. If, on the contrary, my predictions indicate that I will be attacked or humiliated, which would increase my suffering, then I will tend to cut myself off from others when I am suffering and isolate myself.

Thus, the function of a schema is to organize our perception of situations based on the following fundamental questions: **What does this most resemble in my experience, what will happen next, and what is the most adaptive response?** For example, a man with an Abandonment schema who sees his partner talking to another man at an art opening could perceive the following, based on his schema: What does this look like? "At school, I was on my own, my friends let me down." What's going to happen next? "She'll fall in love with him and let me down just like them." What's the best response to that? "I'm going to tell that guy to leave my wife alone."

Understanding these predictive interactions concerning our ability to deal with a threat allows us to understand the coherence of our reactions when, at first glance, they might seem surprising. For instance, in the case of clients with low self-esteem whose view of themselves we would so like to change. People who grow up in a dysfunctional family often blame themselves for relationship breakdowns because perceiving situations more realistically would be unbearable. It is devastating for a child to face a reality in which their parents do not love them. By repeating to themselves that it is their fault (self-denigrating speech), the person can feel like there is a possibility they can do better; the person thus moves from an external locus of control to an internal locus of control. Very often, attitudes of this type (self-denigration, self-blame) reflect this shift from an external locus of control to an internal locus of control. "Next time, I'll be better. I'm going to be so nice that she won't be able to reject me anymore." "I'm going to be hyper-vigilant so I can sense what he wants to talk about, what he wants to do, and he won't reject me." The function of strategies like this is always to ensure survival. According to our model, these strategies are functional for the individual, even if another part of the self understands that they are not serving them. When a person does not understand why they engage in these self-denigrating behaviors and attitudes, we can explain to them that their rational side knows that the strategies are self-defeating and do not need to be convinced. We can help them understand that since the rational side has not been able to change things despite what it observes, it will be more profitable to address the schema, which is still clinging to this self-aggression strategy as a solution to the predicted relationship breakdown.

The more central and crucial a prediction is to the individual's survival, the more tenacious it will be. However, the principle remains the same: When the person explicitly experiences something they cannot interpret from the perspective of their schema, the schema will have to be revisited, updated, and rewritten in a different form in their memory (through the therapeutic memory reconsolidation process, which happens naturally in the brain and that we can bring about intentionally in psychotherapy).

Before moving on to tertiary processes, we would like to present an interesting distinction made by Panksepp (Panksepp & Biven, 2012) between tertiary and primary-secondary processes. He refers to the latter as "intentions-in-action," in the sense that before the appearance of tertiary processes in evolution, a subjective state automatically led to action without any system being able to intervene between the two; this corresponds to the subjective experience of "I can't help it." Tertiary processes, on the other hand, allow another level of control to emerge (Not that it's always effective!): we can consciously experience the "intention to act," which adds the potential option of inhibiting the act. In our view, this is the locus of intervention targeted by many psychotherapeutic modalities, such as ACT, Cognitive Therapy, mindfulness, self-compassion, and many others. These modalities seek to maximize the tremendous potential of tertiary processes, but they do not directly target real transformation at the level of secondary processes, where we believe the early maladaptive schemas identified by Young are located.

Panksepp's Tertiary Processes. The tertiary processes enable the brain to take an observer's perspective (mentalization) about the primary and secondary processes. So, for example, if Erika were to say, "This experience I'm feeling is my Defectiveness schema that has just been reactivated" (see example above), she would be experiencing both the reactivation (emotional truth) and the reframing of this experience (cognitive restructuring can have an impact here).

We are now moving away from what we called the limbic brain in our first book and turning our attention to the neocortex, particularly the frontal cortex. Panksepp locates tertiary processes in these structures. Obviously, in well-integrated brain function, all three levels, primary, secondary, and tertiary, work in harmony—the integration of all parts of the brain is what Siegel (2020) describes as mental health. The following explains the nature of tertiary processes.

Firstly, there are the executive functions, which enable us to think and plan with the invaluable support of language. Human beings are endowed with the extraordinary ability to play virtually with their external and internal realities. We can build a house in our heads before laying the first stone, plan the steps of its construction, modify the plans once the work is underway, and so on. We also try to read other people's intentions towards us and imagine different ways of adapting to them. This is a huge addition to what would otherwise be only instinctual, impulsive or conditioned thinking. Our executive functions have made possible the creation of a social and technical world of immense complexity, which in turn requires that we make use of the great flexibility given us by our neocortex.

The frontal-medial regions, on the other hand, allow for emotional regulation. Our subcortical emotional systems are represented in this region, giving us the ability to use them constructively but also giving us the ability to ruminate (there is always a dark side to progress). We can experience affective states without having to automatically act on them. As we will see later on, we use this very ability as a tool to manage schemas with the Mindfulness Flash Card (Cousineau, 2012; Cousineau & Ngô, 2013), mindfulness being a practice whose goal is to increase our capacity for emotional regulation through building our capacity to experience an affective state without acting on it.

Finally, according to Panksepp, the higher functions of working memory enable what we call freedom of choice ("free will"). This level of freedom is open to debate (Sapolsky, 2023; Wegner, 2002), but the fact remains that, free will or not, human beings are at least capable of intervening in their behavioral patterns to modify how they act when they experience a certain affective state. This is Panksepp's "intention-to-act." As mentioned above, many therapies are based on this principle. To illustrate this, we often refer to the title of Susan Jeffers's book (2007), *Feel the Fear ... And Do It Anyway*, which captures the idea that the tertiary system can impact subcortical systems, giving us, at the very least, an impression of free choice over our actions.

The working memory function we have just described relies on another working memory function: voluntarily controlled conscious attention. For instance, you can voluntarily bring your attention back to reading this book when your phone's notifications beckon you to more exciting things (stay with us; we promise it's worth it!).

Now that we've introduced the three levels of brain functioning as conceptualized by Panksepp, we would like to present the following little story to illustrate the levels in action in a situation familiar to many.

Imagine yourself wanting to take up jogging but, unfortunately, you are one of those people who do not experience runner's high. If you only had a primary process, you would stop running after a few meters, feeling how heavy and painful your legs are and how hard it is to breathe; you would stop because the exercise would be very unpleasant, and no other process would be giving you any reason to continue. Unless a bear were after you, which would give you a very good reason to keep running! Your FEAR system would push you to continue making the effort to run (you would forget your physical pain as your conscious attention would be temporarily mobilized elsewhere).

To illustrate the secondary system, let us say that your family has strongly instilled in you the value of perseverance and the belief that people who take the easy way out are cowards. This secondary process would ensure that you maintained your effort. When the painful sensations of running started to hit, while your primary system would suggest you stop, your secondary system would tell you that if you stopped, it would mean you were a coward. You would, therefore, continue to run because the physical discomfort would be less painful than the pain your internal Punitive Critic mode would inflict.

Finally, a tertiary system, which would be optimal and healthy (Healthy Adult mode), could manifest itself as follows: you feel pain in your legs, you have difficulty breathing, your primary system tells you to stop, but your tertiary system suggests to you without brusqueness or harshness that the option of continuing to run is preferable for your health to that of stopping your exercise, allowing you to continue running despite the pain. ACT, for example, follows the lines of the last scenario: respecting our commitment to our values without engaging in experiential avoidance. In summary, the activity of running, as with any activity, will be dealt with differently depending on the level of the process engaged.

Two Types of Symptom-Generating Memory

We hope we have made clear for you the role that learning—and therefore memory—plays in schema construction because a good understanding of these processes is a major asset to therapeutic work. To further add to your understanding of learning and memory processes, we present in the following paragraphs two types of memory that you will regularly encounter in your practice, each of which has its specificities in terms of interventions to use.

Episodic Memory. In everyday language, what people are usually referring to when they use the word memory is episodic. This is the memory of "episodes" in our lives, from the ordinary memory (what I had for lunch) to the traumatic memory (being attacked in the street). And as every event in our lives has its emotional tone, from the mildest to the most intense, the explicit and present reactivation of a moment in our lives will always be accompanied by an affective experience. When Proust finds himself at his aunt Léonie's in his imagination (associations with tea and madeleines), he is in his episodic memory; in his case, the memory is very pleasant. When I (PC) see the Indian cobra again, the memory is always unpleasant.

Episodic memory is a subjective reactivation in the here and now of previous events in our lives, from a few seconds ago to as far back as we can remember. Initially, the discomfort (PC) in front of the school's metal fence was not coming from episodic memory; it was implicit (felt without the explicit context); it became an episodic memory when the image of sticking our tongues on the fence in the cold winter resurfaced; the author felt like he was there again and at the same time knew that it was the memory of an event that happened in his past.

When we are using our emotional episodic memory, it is like virtually moving back in time. This is the type of memory we draw on when we use mental imagery to revisit moments in our client's life. This enables several discoveries, such as the meaning that was given to a certain event, while at the same time allowing us to work with the memory as it is being reactivated.

In memory reconsolidation, our interventions generally focus on implicit semantic memory, which we will describe shortly, but episodic memory may also require direct intervention. For instance, when its reactivation creates an intolerable level of intensity from which we seek to dissociate ourselves, as is often the case with traumatic memories.

Finally, it is the integration of all our episodic memories into a single scenario in which we are the main actor (we are at the heart of all these events) that forms the autobiographical memory, the one in which we create our conscious identity.

Implicit Semantic Memory. This is the most important type of memory to understand in the context of schema work. We experience events, and from these, most often through statistical learning, we create prototypes/patterns/rules/mental models/schemas that will enable us in the future to recognize what we are experiencing in real-time. What does this look like, and what is going to happen? The answers to these questions lie in implicit semantic memory[10]—the type of memory that serves the predictive function of memory. Bruce Ecker (Ecker et al., 2024) defines semantic memory as follows:

> It turns out to be demonstrable unambiguously in therapy sessions that the vast majority of the unwanted patterns or "symptoms" presented by seekers of psychotherapy are generated by the contents of memory—specifically by learned mental models, or schemas, consisting of particular constructs, held in implicit memory, outside of awareness. The brain's completely nonverbal, implicit, yet highly specific meaning-making and modeling of the world is innate and begins very early in life.[…]
>
> Mental models or schemas are perceived patterns generalized and extracted from specific experiences. Such models live in a different memory system from the memory of the original experiences and events, which researchers term episodic memory. Rather, it is semantic memory systems that hold one's learned mental models. The term "memory" in common usage narrowly means only memory of events or facts, but it is schema memory, semantic memory, that matters most for facilitating transformational change in therapy sessions.
>
> (p.6)

Episodic memory, as mentioned above, refers to events and how we have experienced them; we cannot change what happened. On the other hand—and this is a major point—we can modify the mental models or the schemas we have learned based on these events because they are constructs. For example, when Erika perceives that when her partner (or anyone) speaks loudly, she is in danger of being attacked and can't do anything about it, and she falls into a state of absolute powerlessness, that is a model of the world she has constructed, and that model can be changed. We cannot change the events that created the model but, more often than not, the model itself can be transformed.

Schemas are, therefore, predictive models and implicit knowledge because, most of the time, these constructs are not conscious. Through our subjective experience, we create unconscious constructs that tell us how the world works. For example, a Social Isolation schema will prompt a person to anticipate being sidelined in a social situation. So, when they find themselves in a group, and two people are whispering to each other, their schema will immediately predict that they will be excluded. In response, the person will adopt behaviors that enable them to find a solution to the situation they anticipate, often creating self-fulfilling prophecies. By repeating behaviors of withdrawal from social situations, the person will increase the likelihood of being excluded, creating and maintaining a vicious cycle.

Moreover, this implicit aspect of memory reflects adaptation. For example, Erika has formed an attachment wound from her aggressive father; her schema recognizes the sound of the father slamming the door on his return from work, the tone of his voice, and she now perceives her partner's behavior and tone the same way: "I'm in danger! … Now I have to keep quiet, make as little noise as possible, and make myself very small to avoid becoming the target of his aggression." When Erika hears a loud voice or a door slamming, she does not need conscious attention to put herself in threat protection mode. She will make herself very small without even having to think about it.

Compulsive rituals are another excellent example of implicit semantic learning. For instance, an imperative hand-washing ritual that serves to cancel out an anxiety-producing thought about revenge can be understood as a solution to avoid a predicted disaster.

In Schema Therapy, the concept of adaptation refers to executing all strategic solutions (coping styles, coping modes) aimed at avoiding unpleasant subjective states (the equivalent of experiential avoidance in ACT or defense mechanisms in psychodynamics). We will see that these solutions manifest themselves in the strategic modes of Compliant Surrenderer, Protector-Avoidance, and Counterattacker (Overcompensator).

We will then explain why the most effective way to modify strategic modes is to question the predictions (implicit semantic memory) they are the solution to. Erika will no longer need to make herself small if her prediction of powerlessness in the face of an aggressive person has been transformed—she was helpless as a child, but she is no longer helpless today, so there is no longer any need to subjugate herself.

A Definition of Schemas

The early maladaptive schemas identified by Young, which are primarily implicit memories, correspond to themes of subjective reality (emotional truths) found in human beings' experiences. Therefore, for most of us, they form an important part of our subjective experience and behavior.[11]

As we hope to have convinced you in this chapter, schemas are primarily created through a process of interaction between our phylogenetic memory (including temperament) and our experience—or Panksepp's primary and secondary processes.

Now, how to define them? Here is our suggestion.

A schema is an organizational structure of memory that is made of the following:

- somatic sensations, affects, emotions, subjective states
- perceptual biases, rules, mental models, expectations
- action tendencies
- When language is integrated into memory, it is also made of cognitive coherence and coherent narrative construction.

Finally, let us emphasize a point that is fundamental to the purpose of this book.

> The schema is a **predictive organizational structure of memory**, primarily implicit, whose function is to promote adaptation by automating as many perception–action modules as possible.

This Chapter's Main Points

- Epistemologically speaking, this book takes a constructivist approach. Our relationship with reality ("whatever-it-is," McGilchrist) is modulated by constructs based largely on our memory.
- In this book, we refer to phylogenetic memory as the memory transmitted to us by our genes as a result of the evolution of our species. We use the seven primary affective systems identified by Panksepp to describe it. It is through these systems (including temperament) that our fundamental psychological needs manifest themselves.

- Phylogenetic memory is in constant interaction with the environment. Adaptation of the organism requires a memory that takes into account the specificities of these interactions. This is what we call the memory of experience.
- The memory of an experience is based on the basic principle that **this comes with that** and is constructed mainly implicitly. It creates models of reality, both external (world, others) and internal (self). The early maladaptive schemas identified by Young constitute certain categories of these models of reality.
- Once created, schemas have a predictive function: What do I recognize, what is going to happen, and what can I or can't I do about it? The usefulness of the memory of an experience is thus to prepare us for what lies ahead, to manage our energy budget in the most optimal way possible, and to the immense advantage of not having to reassess every situation as if it were new.
- We believe that schemas, implicit semantic memories, operate mainly at the level of what Panksepp calls primary and secondary processes. This explains why they appear true in our subjective experience and why they constitute emotional truths. Our tertiary (cortical) process, on the other hand, has the potential to develop an observational stance concerning our schemas but does not have the power to directly transform them.
- Our definition of schemas: a **predictive organizational structure of memory**, primarily implicit, whose function is to promote adaptation by automating as many perception-action modules as possible.

Notes

1 Iain McGilchrist's whatever-it-is (2021).

2 By "mental activity" we mean the psychic dimension of human functioning, such as thoughts, affects, and sensations. For example, although the hunger mechanism relies largely on hypothalamus regulation, the sensation of hunger will be experienced as a subjective reality (Leng, 2018). The term is therefore not limited to simple cognitive activity.

3 We referred to this concept by Lisa F Barrett (2018) in our first book (Côté & Cousineau, 2022). Basically, the brain must manage our energy budget by seeking to balance energy expenditure (energy needed to run, to use our working memory to calculate mentally, etc.) with energy intake (eating, resting, being reassured, sleeping, etc.) as best it can. This concept is all the more relevant in the context of early maladaptive schemas, all of which are associated with some form of threat to the individual: What is the resource-to-threat ratio, and what are the consequences for the individual's energy budget?

4 Panksepp uses capital letters to distinguish these basic emotional systems (brain/ mind) from the use of these same words in everyday language.
5 Desire and need satisfaction are two well-identified neuropsychological systems (Lewis, 2015).
6 In Canada today, many disapprove of the use of this term, which is associated with the era of colonialism. Instead, we use the terms “Indigenous” or “First Nations.”
7 “When an axon of cell A is near enough to excite a cell B and repeatedly or persistently takes part in firing it, some growth process or metabolic change takes place in one or both cells such that A’s efficiency, as one of the cells firing B, is increased” (p. 62).
8 In Search of Lost Time.
9 “No sooner had I recognized the taste of the crumb of sponge-cake dipped in lime tea that my aunt used to give me (although why the memory should make me so happy I still had no idea; and I would have to postpone finding this out until much later) than the old grey house with her bedroom in it and the street outside appeared and was joined like scenery to the little wing built for my parents overlooking the back garden (which was the isolated segment I had always remembered); and not only the house, but the village at all hours of the day and in all weathers, the Square where I was sent to play before lunch, the streets where I ran errands and the lanes round about where we walked if it was fine. And, just as in that Japanese game where you have a bowl of water into which you dip tiny pieces of nondescript paper which instantly begin to stretch and open, taking on color, dimension and bulk, turning into flowers or houses or recognizable characters, so there and then all the flowers in our garden and in M. Swann’s grounds, the water-lilies on the Vivonne, the local people in their little houses, the church and all of Combray town with its gardens and countryside took shape and body and rose up out of my cup of tea” (Swann’s Way, p. 45).
10 It is important to note that Tulving’s (1972) model of semantic memory concerns explicit memory.
11 This assertion is based on a consensus among many clinicians, and on studies that have at least demonstrated the therapeutic usefulness of these concepts. From a constructivist point of view, this does not refer to what could be considered an objective truth. But for us, early maladaptive schemas are a conviction that is repeatedly supported in our clinical and everyday reality.

Chapter 2
Modes

We can tell that someone is sad, angry, stressed, withdrawn, intrusive without knowing what is making them feel or behave that way. What do you think is the best way to find out what is prompting the feeling or behavior?

Our answer is to work with the person to discover what predictions are activated and causing the reactions we are observing. For example, if we observe that a person is in a state of terror and urgently searching for protection, we could discover that these reactions stem from an apprehension of aggressive reprisals from someone close to that person.

This reflects the relationship between modes and schemas. The schema is the prediction, and the mode is the response to the prediction, mobilized by the organism. This response takes place at several levels: physiological, affective, kinesthetic, motor, verbal, and so forth. Understandably, it is easier to have direct access to the response than to the implicit prediction that underlies it. This is why the presence of a mode is our first indication that an issue has been triggered.

However, in Schema Therapy (ST) training courses, modes are often the most difficult concept for participants to grasp. Whereas schemas can be conceptualized on the basis of categorical criteria, the identification of modes relies more on an overall impression of the state in which the person is immersed. In the spirit of McGilchrist (2009, 2021), we would say that the identification of modes requires greater right–hemisphere, left–hemisphere integration on the part of the therapist. It is precisely with the intention of fostering this integration that the following exercise has been designed for use in training. It is based on a story created around a person with an Abandonment schema.

DOI: 10.4324/9781003628125-3

The following is the scenario we present at the beginning of the exercise.

Introduction to the Exercise

There is a couple in which the wife has a strong Abandonment schema. She fears that her husband will become interested in another woman and cheat on her. One of the main strategies she uses to prevent this from happening is to try to control his schedule as much as possible to ensure that he is continually under her surveillance. She also checks his cell phone while he is showering to ensure it does not contain messages from another woman. Her need for control is triggered particularly intensely when her husband mentions his company Christmas party: he says he has to attend. His participation in this annual event, which arouses such apprehension in her, gives rise to intense negotiations between them as to the time he is "allowed" to spend at the party. After bitter discussions, they come to agree that he will be home from the party by midnight at the latest.

The Exercise

It is the evening of the Christmas party. Monsieur (husband) has already left, and Madame (wife) is home alone.

11:30: Monsieur has not returned—the agreement has not yet been broken, but Madame would have liked him to return before midnight, out of consideration for her feelings. She is disappointed.

Midnight: Monsieur is not back home yet.

12:30 … 1:00 … 1:30 … Monsieur still has not returned.

The following question is now put to the participants in the training workshop: What are your guesses about the state Madame would find herself in at 1:30 a.m.?

We suggest you make your own guess before reading further and seeing the answers we regularly receive in our training workshops.

Here is a sample of answers regularly received in workshops: panic, anger, rage, distress, terrorized, upset, sadness, despair, helplessness, fear, annoyed, resigned, downcast, restless, empty, crying, super tense, great internal tension, frustration, disappointment, explosion (breaking things).

The interesting thing about this exercise is that the answers are generated entirely by the participants and are therefore totally based on their perception of reality, and not on that of the trainer. One of us (PC) has been using this exercise for some twenty years, in several countries around the world and with different cultures.[1] And the answers are always the same! The Abandonment schema is the person's fear of a lack of response to a fundamental psychological need, that of relational stability with people who are particularly significant. Yet, without necessarily knowing it at a conceptual level, the participants are able to identify the two fundamental types of reactions prompted when **a fundamental psychological need is not met,** according to ST: Vulnerable Child and Angry Child modes.

Why "Child" modes? Because the reactivation of an early maladaptive schema manifests itself in the form in which it was learned; it is simply a reactivation of memory that has not been updated at a later age. And, if you refer back to Chapter 1, you will remember that we believe the early maladaptive schemas identified by Young correspond to Panksepp's primary and secondary level systems, or subcortical responses. Moreover, in everyday life, if a man sulks whenever something does not suit him, we use the phrase "he acts like a child." Conversely, the Healthy Adult mode—which will be further discussed later in this section—requires harmony between cortical and subcortical functioning, and effective regulation of our emotional markers.

And what is the difference between the Vulnerable Child and Angry Child modes? When a fundamental psychological need is not adequately met, the organism is threatened. And the primary affective systems activated in these situations are FEAR—PANIC/GRIEF—RAGE (ANGER). If you review the answers given by the participants in our exercise, you will find that they correspond to these three systems and their close derivatives. Obviously, the FEAR and PANIC/GRIEF systems form the basis of the Vulnerable Child mode, and the RAGE (ANGER) system is the basis of the Angry Child mode.

Let's look at how the answers to our exercise with the Abandonment schema correspond to each mode.

Vulnerable Child mode: panic, distress, terrorized, upset, sadness, despair, helplessness, fear, resignation, downcast, restless, empty, crying, super tense, great internal tension, disappointment.

Angry Child mode: anger, rage, annoyance, frustration, explosion (breaking things).

What the affective systems characterizing the Vulnerable Child and Angry Child modes have in common is that they constitute unpleasant experiences. They indicate to the organism that something is wrong and prompt it to produce a response, either by calling on external resources or by using its internal resources. At the time of their creation, early maladaptive schemas are based on the following equation: External resources are either insufficient or inappropriate, and internal resources are not sufficient, at this stage of life, to ensure an adequate response to basic psychological needs. This leads the organism to deregulate and adopt rigid or chaotic solutions (Siegel, 2020).

Conclusion of the Exercise

Let's return to our Abandonment schema scenario. It is now 1:30 a.m. and Monsieur has not yet returned. Madame's anxiety level has become intolerable. If, according to the ST model, she adopts dysfunctional coping strategies, this is what it might look like.

- She pours herself several glasses of Scotch to numb her suffering ("drowning her pain")—Protector-Avoidance mode.
- Or, convinced that her spouse has cheated on her, she puts on make-up, puts on her sexiest dress, goes to a bar and picks up a man with whom she has extramarital sex—Overcompensator mode.
- Or, although she is experiencing intense anger, she chooses not to express it when her partner finally returns home (at 2 a.m.), and she feigns interest in how his night went—Compliant Surrenderer mode.

These three modes are strategic; their function is to prevent direct contact with psychological suffering perceived as intolerable and unmanageable by the nervous system: using the "means at hand" at the time of their creation. At the time of their adoption as strategic modes, they constituted the best solution available to the individual, given the context in which they were learned (available external and internal resources). However, in therapy, we refer to them as dysfunctional because they have become obstacles to the full development of the person, who implicitly chooses flight (avoidance), rather than confronting their problems. To find healthier solutions, the person needs to confront their problems instead of engaging in avoidance. The way we refer to this process in ST is replacing these dysfunctional strategic modes with a Healthy Adult mode.

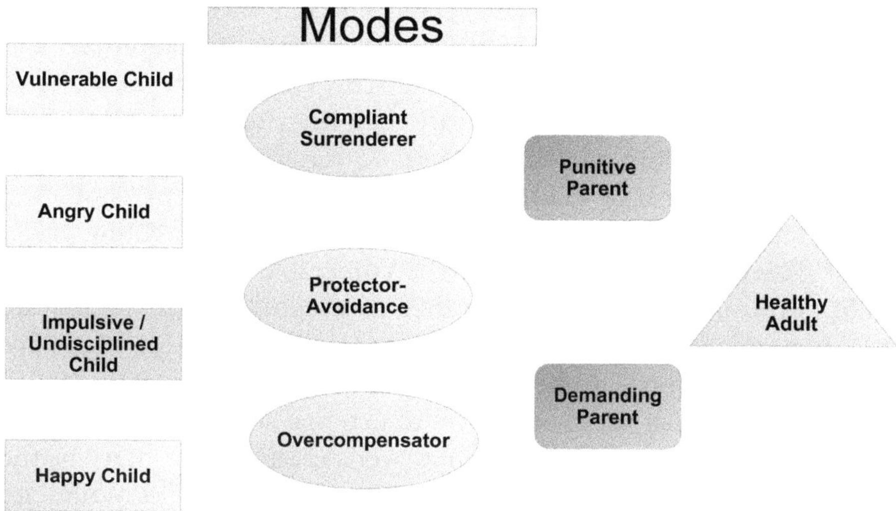

Figure 2.1 *Modes*

In his original model, Young (Young et al., 2003) identified ten modes. Later, sub-modes were refined (Arntz et al., 2013; Brockman et al., 2023; Edwards, 2022; Jacob & Arntz, 2021), leading to +20 modes. In our basic schema training courses, we choose to present the original ten-mode model. This ensures that participants are not overloaded with concepts, as well as ensuring the fullest possible integration of the fundamental paradigms of the mode model. Once this initial integration is complete, it becomes easy for the therapist to add the sub-modes to their work.

Our exercise with the lady with the Abandonment schema is a way to give a first introduction to the concept of modes. The ten basic modes we will be working with are listed in Figure 2.1. We give definitions of these modes in the following paragraphs.

Child Modes

There are four "Child" modes. We pointed out earlier that the term "Child" refers to the reactivation of a memory in the form in which it exists in the emotional memory. Here, we are referring to early schemas acquired when we were children. The first two modes, Vulnerable Child Mode and Angry Child mode, are pivotal in ST. Why? Because they indicate where the response to a fundamental psychological need is insufficient or absent, and we can therefore rely on them to identify what is missing or underdeveloped in the person who is in therapy. Young et al. (2003) emphasizes the fundamental links between his approach and attachment theory (Cassidy & Shaver, 2016). However, in the majority of cases, work on needs requires more than psychoeducation on needs and their universality and importance. It requires experiential work involving some form of validation of those fundamental psychological needs (Jacob & Arntz, 2021; van der Wijngaart, 2021; Young et al., 2003). This explains why we refer to the Vulnerable Child and the Angry Child as pivotal modes. A schema therapist regularly seeks to activate these two modes, that are often buried under strategic modes that have become dysfunctional, to help the person find adequate responses to their needs now that they have access to external and internal resources that were absent when their schemas were created. The parts of the self that constitute the Vulnerable Child and Angry Child modes are always awaiting a process of completion (Levine, 1997, 2010), or of mourning in contexts where completion is impossible (Stark, 2017). In this sense, they constitute the intentionality on which the therapeutic process will seek to build—fundamentally—the aspiration to change must depend on the motivation of the person consulting, not on yours as a therapist! And it is the engagement with the Vulnerable Child and Angry Child modes that fosters that motivation: **Here's what I'm missing and what I need. Here's what's unacceptable to me and what needs to change**.

Vulnerable Child Mode. When a situation activates the Vulnerable Child mode, it means that the person is experiencing suffering associated with the fact that one of their fundamental psychological needs is not being sufficiently met. The Vulnerable Child mode is characterized by direct contact with this suffering. Solms (2015, 2021) points out that the function of affective consciousness is to assign valence to experience: "They [feelings] are how we become aware of our drives; they tell us how well or badly things are going in relation to the specific needs they measure."[2] The suffering associated with the Vulnerable Child mode thus points to an imbalance within the person's bio-affective system (see Chapter 1), and ST aims to help the person learn to correct this imbalance using their internal resources and adequate external resources; this therapeutic result is what we call the Healthy Adult mode.

And what are the "biological value systems" involved in the Vulnerable Child mode? Regarding Panksepp's model presented in Chapter 1, we opt for the following two primary affective systems, PANIC/GRIEF and FEAR. The vulnerability paradigm suits them well.

Now, what are basic psychological needs according to ST? They are needs that are in line with the main principles of attachment, autonomy and self-control, healthy self-image and self-expression.

At the beginning of life and during childhood, responses to these needs rely essentially on external resources, particularly parental figures. The following is a list of the main basic psychological needs: affection, love, connection, stability of connection, protection, respect, empathy, acceptance, validation, support for the gradual development of autonomy. Added to this is the need for supervision and limits, which will be discussed later on.

Here is a sample of qualifiers that can be used to describe the subjective state of a person in Vulnerable Child mode: deprived, misunderstood, alone, panicked, frightened, feeling miserable, excluded, directionless, anxious, distressed, suffering, helpless, discouraged, hopeless, and so forth.

When a child learns from experience that a need has little or no chance of being met, their memory will make a rule out of it, leading them to predict that this is how relationships work. A schema has been created. For example, I cannot expect a person to remain interested in staying in a stable relationship with me (which is the case of the lady with an Abandonment schema described in the exercise). When this prediction is activated, when it becomes a perception, it can trigger the Vulnerable Child mode, one of the two options at the primary level. The other option is Angry Child mode, which is the mode we describe next.

Angry Child Mode. Vulnerable Child and Angry Child modes are like two sides of the same coin. Vulnerable Child mode emerges when the person is in direct contact with the suffering caused by an unmet basic psychological need, and Angry Child mode is a refusal, a revolt against this situation: It is intolerable, should not be, and must change.

We are now dealing with Panksepp's RAGE system, which can be observed in its pure state in very young children. With no secondary or tertiary control yet developed, a young child can bite or hit a sibling who has suddenly become a rival for Mom's attention. As we saw in the previous chapter, if the RAGE system is not socialized to foster appropriate expression of anger (healthy assertiveness), the child who is now an adult is at risk of serious personal and social maladjustments that may even lead to troubles with the law. But even when socialized into adaptive anger in a mature person, the RAGE system can still express itself vehemently in certain contexts—think of the snarl many of us can display when we swat a mosquito that has just bitten us (totally unacceptable)!

Like the Vulnerable Child mode, the Angry Child mode is triggered by an inadequate response to a fundamental psychological need. However, the RAGE system pushes us to confront this reality, to demand change. The RAGE system causes the mobilization of energy that motivates us to refuse the status quo, which does not meet our needs. With the right internal and external resources, this motivational system can foster the affirmation and willingness to change what is wrong in the person's situation—for example, by putting an end to an abusive relationship. However, when the person is in Angry Child mode, they have become stuck in the reactivation of this implicit semantic memory, still in its early, primary form, which is now inappropriate in their current life context. For example, an intense tantrum from a spouse because his partner has been somewhat slow to respond to him (Emotional Deprivation schema), blaming her for never listening to what he says. This manifestation of Angry Child mode will certainly not foster a healthy relationship. Here, again, popular language captures this mode very well when an individual is said to "act like a child."

As we did for the Vulnerable Child mode, we provide here a sample of qualifiers that can be used to describe the subjective state of a person in Angry Child mode: disgruntled, impatient, annoyed, upset, irritated, frustrated, angry, exasperated, explosive, furious, and so forth.

When the expression of anger becomes explosive, such as when a person hits others or breaks things, Arntz et al. (2013) refer to this state as the Enraged Child mode. This is an example of a mode added to Young's original model by other authors. As we pointed out earlier, these additional modes are refinements of the original model and do not fundamentally challenge it.

The Angry Child mode manifests itself in reactivity to given contexts. We will see later on that anger can also be part of the Protector-Avoidance or Overcompensator modes, but it will be used strategically rather than expressed in a reactive manner in situations where there is a perceived obstacle preventing response to a fundamental psychological need.

It is reasonable to say that, with regard to the Angry Child mode, the aim of ST is to help the person in therapy recover the motivational energy that comes from this mode and use it in the service of their legitimate needs. For the energy to be used effectively to answer the person's needs, it must be done in an adapted, context-sensitive way, rather than in a way that usually results in a negative response from the environment because its expression is deemed brutal or socially unacceptable, such as behaviors rooted in the Angry Child mode.

Impulsive/Undisciplined Child Mode. In the Angry Child mode, anger can be expressed explosively, but this anger is always in relation to what is perceived as an unanswered fundamental psychological need. It is not the case with the "Impulsive" component of the Impulsive/Undisciplined mode. It "responds to urges, impulses, cravings, and wants in an impulsive, uncontrolled way, without consideration of the medium—and longer-term impact on themselves and others" (Brockman et al., 2023, p. 7). The person in this mode could say something like "I want it and I will not be refused"—intense anger can be aroused by anything that stands in the way of this expectation. It is the Entitlement schema that most often activates the "Impulsive" part of this Child mode.

On the other hand, the "Undisciplined" facet of this mode expresses itself in the form of intolerance to the frustrations caused by the discipline that is necessary for the smooth running of daily life or the achievement of medium- or long-term objectives. For example, tolerating the boredom of domestic chores to ensure the proper upkeep of a living space, or depriving oneself of repeated outings with friends to bars to study for a university degree.

This mode corresponds to a further dimension of child development. Of course, children need love, validation and support in developing their autonomy, but they also need supervision to help them integrate limits and establish self-control. Functioning both socially and individually requires a capacity to control one's behavior, to consider others in one's decisions, and the ability to set and achieve personal goals.

When there is impulsivity in ADD/ADHD, it is important to carry out a sufficiently thorough assessment to determine to what extent the impulsivity is learned, and to what extent it is attributable to neurodivergence. A person suffering from ADD/ADHD may have experiences that lead to learnings that exacerbate the impulsivity already attributable to the neurodevelopmental divergence. Therapeutic intervention can only modify encodings resulting from learning, not symptoms attributable to a neurological condition.

Happy Child Mode. Like the Healthy Adult mode, the Happy Child mode is a healthy state and activating it is a goal to be achieved, not a problem. When a child is fortunate enough to grow up in optimal educational conditions, they feel loved, protected, accepted, understood, valued, guided in their progress towards autonomy, safe, and in control, which generates feelings of satisfaction, calm, confidence and optimism. Such a child would have all the support needed to express their spontaneity, that self-generated strength so readily observable in infancy and that is another essential aspect of this mode. When a child develops in optimal conditions, no one needs to make them take an interest in their surroundings, to discover and to interact with their surroundings. The SEEKING system simply actualizes itself in a sea of things to be known and mastered. That is why we also use the term Spontaneous Child mode.

And, of course, it is unlikely that such a child would ever need to go for psychotherapy. Then why do we need this mode in ST? Any contact adults have with their own spontaneity will always be a plus for their motivational system, leading them to make choices that are in harmony with who they are on a deeper level, rather than acting to avoid punishment or rejection, for example (the Subjugation schema—more on this in the next chapter). Ryan and Deci (2017) have long demonstrated the considerable impact of intrinsic motivation (self-determination) on a human being's level of well-being. The schema therapist should therefore pay close attention to everything that emerges spontaneously in the patient and help them to become aware of it and learn to rely on this powerful personal compass.

As the Happy Child mode is one of the Child modes, this means that the person consulting does not yet possess sufficient internal resources to function autonomously. They need help from external resources to temper their spontaneity with reality. For example, a three-year-old girl running after her ball in the street needs parental supervision. Once she has developed the ability to self-supervise using her own internal resources, we would consider that her spontaneity is being exercised in Healthy Adult mode.

Dysfunctional Strategic (Coping) Modes

If there is one point on which many therapeutic systems can agree without too much difficulty, it is that human beings (like many animals for that matter) do not like to suffer; it is a "biological value" as Solms

(2015, 2021) would emphasize. In the deep, archaic layers of the brain, there are structures, such as the now-famous periaqueductal gray matter, the PAG (Damasio, 1999; Panksepp & Biven, 2012; Solms, 2021), that have been working for millennia to help us avoid pain and suffering. As you now understand, Vulnerable Child and Angry Child modes generate suffering; they are affective markers of the absence of adequate responses to fundamental psychological needs. They are therefore linked to the organism's survival structures. For example, a newborn baby left alone would simply not survive, hence, the absolute necessity for the organism to be able to signal the situation forcefully via the PANIC/GRIEF system. But if the suffering is not quickly relieved, the organism will begin to protect itself from the suffering itself. That is the function of the strategic modes called "dysfunctional" in ST. These strategies become dysfunctional as the person's situation changes, but they were functional when they developed because they were the only solutions available at the time, given the child's limited external and internal resources.

We highlighted the use of the terms "lesser" and "worse" suffering in our book on Coherence Therapy (Côté & Cousineau, 2022). These terms apply to the reality we are describing here as well. The lesser suffering is caused by the person's protective strategies; for example, all the consequences associated with anorexia, which can even be life-threatening. So why the term "lesser" when this suffering can be so intense? Because it is always a question of perception: The suffering that would come with the feared consequence of not using the strategy appears even worse to the person than what they are imposing on their body. Extreme examples like anorexia can help to understand why Barrett's (2018) term "everyday hallucinations," or Seth's (2021) "controlled hallucinations" are not as extreme as one might think! In the case of a patient suffering from severe anorexia, their "hallucination" can lead to serious health problems, even death.

Because they have become dysfunctional, strategic modes are often the reason why people seek help. Either because the cost of the strategy has become prohibitive (e.g., extreme submission has led the person to ignore their interests to the point that life has lost all meaning); or because the strategy no longer works (e.g., alcohol no longer gives relief from a deep sense of emptiness).

We mentioned earlier that schema therapists often work with the Vulnerable Child and Angry Child modes. Dysfunctional strategic modes are therefore seen as an obstacle to be overcome to reach these

Child modes. The parallel with psychodynamic approaches' defense mechanisms learned during childhood is obvious. Young often mentions how, because he was first associated with cognitive-behavioral therapy, he was regularly criticized in the early days for overemphasizing the importance of childhood learning. If this question is an issue for you, we suggest the following perspective. Imagine a person who has grown up in a dysfunctional family, and this person develops significant schemas such as Abandonment, Emotional Deprivation, Mistrust/Abuse, and so forth. Then, let's imagine that they leave their family at the age of 18 and say to themselves something like this: What I've learned so far reflects the environment in which I've lived. Now, I'm going to go out and discover the world, to find out how it works, and I'm going to create new mental models, new schemas, about the way it all works. If things could work out that way, then we would not have to worry about how these schemas or strategies were created. Unfortunately, it does not work that way. When we see, for example, women ending up again and again with abusive partners, or how it is impossible for many to stop a compulsive behavior through sheer willpower, we may wonder why their programming can't simply be changed. If we could modify human operating systems the way we change our telephone and computer systems, things would be very different!

In Young's original model (2003), there were three dysfunctional strategic modes. They are as follows.

Compliant Surrenderer Mode. Childhood is the period of life when external resources are most essential. Children cannot cope on their own so parents play a crucial role in the child's world. This is why losing parents, alienating them, or having to deal with their anger and rejection would be a considerable threat. The solution? Make sure this does not happen. The Compliant Surrenderer mode serves to maintain the connection with the care-taking other by:

- Behaving in such a way that the other person does not reject us or get angry with us.
- Focusing on the other person's needs and trying to meet them.
- Developing extreme sensitivity to detect the other person's expectations of us and conforming to them to avoid disappointing them and to win their approval.

These three strategies correspond to three schemas: Subjugation, Self-Sacrifice, and Approval-Seeking schemas.

People with a Compliant Surrenderer mode adjust to the context. They do not easily challenge, oppose or question. When they do, it is likely because they are actually complying with a group that is challenging, opposing or questioning! In everyday life, these people can more easily be controlled, used and even exploited by others. Also, when they apply these strategies to the point where they never consider what is really important to them, they run the risk of presenting certain problems without seeing the connection with their conciliation behaviors, such as a lack of personal direction, lack of interest in life, and psychosomatic problems.

What's more, they tend to be submissive patients, attributing inordinate power to the therapist. The challenge is to create a context in which they can take the risk of being themselves.

Protector-Avoidance Mode.[3] Protector-Avoidance mode is expressed in all strategies aimed at reducing the emotional intensity associated with direct contact with basic suffering (the "worse" suffering). Under the control of this mode, the individual will seek to cut themself off from what they feel or fear feeling. This is probably the mode with the widest range of manifestations, but the function is always the same: to reduce affective intensity and, in some cases, to cut oneself off completely from affect, the most extreme form being total dissociation.

Here are some examples of Protector-Avoidance mode:

- Behavioral avoidance: avoiding certain places, people, situations, and so forth.
- Emotional avoidance: The Emotional Inhibition schema leads individuals to avoid contact with their emotions. For example, they are very rational, cold, they intellectualize, and so forth.
- Soothing through the use of substances such as drugs or alcohol.
- Escape into another form of intensity such as hypersexuality, bulimia, or extreme sports.
- Systematic minimization of what is experienced; "it's not serious … it's not important."
- Somatization: The body ends up signaling a nonmentalized malaise.
- Dissociation.

We mentioned earlier that, in our opinion, the modes subsequently added to the ten basic modes defined by Young are actually sub-modes in relation to the initial model. However, there is one that we find particularly relevant to clinical work: the Angry Protector mode (Arntz et al., 2013; Brockman et al., 2023). Here, anger is not a reaction to the absence of an adequate response to a basic psychological need, but rather serves as a protective wall against what is perceived as an outside threat. For example, when a person perceives intimacy as a threat, this mode will serve to repel anyone who seeks to get emotionally close to the person or who may witness the person's vulnerability in a given context. Anger is used here to repel a perceived threat.

Overcompensator Mode. In Overcompensator mode, which we also call Counter-Attacker mode, the person does not opt for submission or flight but rather chooses to attack the problem head-on. In ST, the conceptualization of the narcissistic personality is a classic example (Behary, 2021; Young, 2003). The need to present oneself as exceptional, and to force the other person to recognize it, has the function of compensating for the opposite feeling, that is, the conviction of being uninteresting, pathetic, or contemptible. This requires constant effort.

The Counter-Attacker acts forcefully because being in a position of vulnerability, powerlessness or victimhood is out of the question (again, the "worst": suffering). For example, becoming an expert in a scientific specialty (Unrelenting Standards schema), to protect oneself from being ignored or humiliated in exchanges with colleagues. Maintaining this position of expertise will also require significant investments of time and energy, which could have a negative impact ("lesser" suffering) on health and quality of relationships.

The Overcompensator mode can have an advantage over the Compliant Surrenderer and Protector-Avoidance modes, as it often increases a person's pool of internal resources. This is obvious in the case of our scientific specialist. The position is an active one, closer to the basic biological response of "attack," the one that serves to confront problems. As with all dysfunctional strategies, however, the problem never really gets solved, and the apprehension of the worse suffering (Vulnerable Child and Angry Child modes) always hovers in the background. What if the narcissist is no longer admired, or the perfectionist pushes themself to the point of burnout? As we often point out, if the strategies were flawless, these people would not come to us for help.

As we have seen, the Overcompensator mode is active; under its influence, the person seeks to control the situation. As the two last examples illustrate, this is usually done by adopting a style of behavior that is opposite to the one the basic schema would lead the person to adopt (the "worse" suffering), hence, the term Counter-Attacker. A jealous person who spies on their spouse for fear of being abandoned if they miss a clue, a person with a low sense of self-worth aiming to become a star on social media (many "followers" = I'm valuable), a counter-phobic who faces their fear, an individual constantly controlling those around them to prevent the chaos experienced in their family of origin, a bully whose mental model is based on "better to attack than to be attacked," and so on. In each of these examples, we can sense the type of problem that is likely to accompany the solution. For example, for the jealous person who is abandoned because their spouse can no longer tolerate being so closely watched, modes and schemas can lead to self-fulfilling prophecies.

Maladaptive Inner Critic (Parent) Modes

These modes take two distinct forms: Punitive Parent and Demanding Parent. According to ST, these modes are created when the child directly internalizes the parent's (or other significant figure's) attitudes towards them. It is as if a facet of the parent has become a carbon copy inside the child, and is now, despite its external origin, one of the facets of the child's self. This now internalized Parent mode then finds itself interacting with the other modes; it has become an active player in the person's overall functioning. Think of comments a person might make to themselves, such as, "What a jerk you are!" or "Instead of having fun, you should have used your time more productively by reading scientific articles."

Punitive Parent Mode. Punitive Parent mode manifests as reactions that are extremely harsh, critical, blaming, punitive and aggressive towards oneself. Often, the person has been severely punished for expressing normal needs and feelings or never allowed to make mistakes. It is as if the person's adult life continues to unfold under the gaze of an intolerant critic ready to blame them for aspects of their experience that are actually normal and legitimate on a psychological level.

For example, a person who makes a mistake and angrily calls themself "an idiot and a jerk." Or a person who self-mutilates in response to a reproach from their partner, telling themself, "This is what you deserve." This readiness to punish oneself can even lead to suicidal ideations.

Demanding Parent Mode. In this mode, it is the demands for performance or conduct that are rigid and disproportionate. Here again, the mode is the internalization of the demands made on the child by a parent who had excessive expectations regarding performance in certain domains, the optimal use of time or the attainment of high social positions. These expectations could also concern certain behaviors, such as putting others' needs before one's own, maintaining perfect order, or manifesting excessive humility.

An example illustrating the Demanding Parent mode is provided in the story of a client who was as brilliant in her field of professional practice as she had been in her studies. Both her parents had university careers. While she was still a student, she had the opportunity to attend a prestigious North American university for her doctoral studies. After three months on campus, she could no longer bear the loneliness and distance from her parents and chose to end her enrolment in the prestigious program. She never experienced this as a loss of self-worth—so her Unrelenting Standards schema was not playing a compensatory role (Overcompensator mode). What bothered her was that she had broken a family rule—that of always striving for the most prestigious degree possible in your field of study (Demanding Parent mode).

A classic intervention with maladaptive Inner Critic modes in ST is to get the client to confront, to oppose, this parental position that has become part of them. Often, the therapist will have first confronted the parent themselves in imagery, providing a reassuring experience for the client and serving as a model. For example, van der Wijngaart (2021) proposes an experiential technique of imagery rescripting, while Jacob and Arntz (2021) describe experiential techniques of chairwork. This type of intervention with maladaptive parenting modes provides us with the opportunity to achieve our goal of integrating memory reconsolidation into ST. When, in Coherence Therapy, we work to reconsolidate memory, we always stress the importance of making the implicit coherence of a symptom explicit. We would therefore seek to understand what makes it necessary for a person to maintain this "solution" of self-punishment or inordinate demands. We never oppose the subjective need to produce the symptom, but rather work to create conditions that will allow for an update of the subjective memory that makes it necessary for the person to maintain their solution despite all the inconveniences it causes. We invite you to stay with us to see what we can do to address this dilemma between opposing the symptom and making sense of its coherence.

Healthy Adult Mode

In the language of ST, a person consults us when their modes cause them to suffer (e.g., the feeling of exclusion in Vulnerable Child mode) or leads them to behave in a way that is ultimately counterproductive (e.g., avoidance in Protector-Avoidance mode). These problems stem from a lack of functional integration between solutions and fundamental needs. Therapy aims to favor this integration and to develop a "good enough parent" within the person. The term "good enough parent" refers to the development of sufficient internal resources (including the ability to use appropriate external resources) that will ensure that the person's needs are adequately met. Any progress in this integration increases the space occupied by the Healthy Adult mode. Now, how does this look in the context of clinical intervention?

Let's start by recalling the assumptions we made in Chapter 1. Schemas, and their activation in modes, are mainly registered at the level of Panksepp's primary and secondary systems. They are therefore triggered quickly, usually well before the tertiary system has had a chance to intervene and contextualize the situation. And although they were appropriate solutions in the context in which they were created, they are no longer so in the current context (reason for consultation). To use an image: It is like the emotional brain does not know that the strategy causes problems even though the neocortex may have become aware of it, hence, the familiar "I know it's not good for me, but I can't help it." This awareness allows for two types of intervention to be applied, both aimed at increasing the power of the Healthy Adult mode. Either we seek to create new memories that will oppose the reactivated schema, most often by utilizing neocortical functions (tertiary system), or we aim to modify the implicit semantic memory that is the schema through the therapeutic memory reconsolidation process. The second type of change can be brought about deliberately or not.

Whether we manage or modify the schema, its control over the person's experience and behavior will be considerably reduced. This leads us to the first definition of the Healthy Adult mode: it is the state brought about by a reduction, ideally the elimination, of the influence of one or more schemas on our functioning. Any reduction of the zones of influence of schemas means an extension of those of the mode.

In the Healthy Adult mode, the person can work toward their long-term well-being. It allows the person to make wise decisions, whereas dysfunctional strategies are aimed at immediate, ad hoc avoidance of perceived threats. What's more, the perceptions of threat have not been updated by integrating current resources and knowledge, which does not allow for an efficient use of our energy budget. Think of a person who is intolerant of any form of contact with sadness, and who engages in compulsive eating as an avoidance strategy whenever sadness appears. All this energy expenditure does nothing to improve the person's self-fulfillment. But if a therapeutic intervention were to raise the person's level of tolerance to discomfort through the use of mindfulness techniques, thus creating a reflexive space for more appropriate choices to be made, or if a genuine modification of the schema's predictions were made possible (integration of external and internal resources now available for coping with sadness), this would enable the Healthy Adult mode to take control of a significant part of the energy budget and use it in the service of achieving greater personal fulfillment.

And, finally, what might an optimal Healthy Adult mode look like? We're often asked this question, but there is no one best answer. However, let's allow ourselves to just express what we think (and enjoy the pleasure of the SEEKING system!). The answer that comes to us would be a person in Spontaneous (Happy) Child mode, that reservoir of vitality, now capable of self-regulation (internal resources), in relationship with others (external resources) while remaining the best judge of the person's own experience. This person could demonstrate both realism and vitality in intimate relationships and other relationships, as well as in the exploration and mastery of their universe. The person would have found an optimal balance between reality and adequate responses to their fundamental psychological needs, including that of caring for others, because they would fully realize that responding to one's needs certainly does not mean being essentially self-centered.

Skiing Exercise

Because modes are a concept often difficult to integrate, we like to conclude this section of our training sessions with a short exercise to have some fun with the concept. We call it "Modes on Skis". We ask participants to think of ten subjective states, one for each mode, in which a person could ski. Our own answers can be found at the end of this chapter.

- Skiing for excitement and pleasure.
- Skiing because you must be in shape.
- Skiing to be the best and be admired.
- Skiing because of subjugation to your spouse.
- Skiing to escape a spouse who does not like to ski.
- Suffering from not performing as well as others on skis.
- Feeling entitled to go ahead of the others while waiting for the lift.
- Yelling at your partner on the way home for being more interested in the other skiers than in you.
- Disproportionately punishing your child for not following your instructions on the slopes.
- A feeling of harmony between fun and technical mastery.

Proust's Way

We mentioned at the very beginning of this chapter that the identification of modes is based on an overall impression of the state in which a person is immersed. Now you may easily imagine that we can quickly switch from one mode to another depending on internal and external contexts. Here we give ourselves the pleasure (in Spontaneous Child mode!) of sharing this excerpt from Marcel Proust's *À la recherche du temps perdu* (*In Search of Lost Time*)*: Du côté de chez Swann* (*Swann's Way*), whose descriptive refinement and poetic writing will more than do justice to these subjective experiences typical of modes (**boldface** ours). You'll also notice all the many schemas that are activated!

> On those walks, I had been able to dream throughout the afternoon of the **pleasures** to be derived from being the friend of the Duchesse de Guermantes, from trout-fishing or drifting down the Vivonne in a boat, and at such moments, in my greed for contentment, **I had wanted life never to be anything but an unbroken sequence of happy afternoons**. But when we were on our way home and I had caught sight of a certain farm, standing to our left a fair distance away from two other farmhouses which were very close together (and from which point, to come back

down into Combray village, all one had to do was walk along an avenue of oaks flanked on one side by small enclosed fields containing regularly spaced out apple-trees whose shadows, in the sunset light, dappled the grass with Japanese patterns), that was the moment when **my heart would miss a beat**—I knew that we would be home within the half-hour, that in accordance with the rule obtaining on days when we walked along the Guermantes way and dinner was served late I would be sent up to bed as soon as I had finished my soup and that **Mama**, sitting on after my departure as though there was company to entertain, **would not be coming up to kiss me good-night in bed**. **The zone of sadness which I had just entered** was as **clearly marked off from the other zone in which only a moment before I had been full of joy** as a strip of pink sky may be separated from a band of green or black as though by a ruled line. One may see a bird flying against the background of pink, nearing the boundary of it, almost touching the band of black—and then it disappears into it. **I was now so removed from the desires I had just been harbouring**—to visit Guermantes, to travel and be happy that even if they had come true there and then **I could have derived no enjoyment from their realization**. How I longed to give them all for one night spent sobbing in Mama's arms! **I shuddered, unable to tear my anxious eyes away from the face of my mother** who was not going to come to my bedroom tonight, and, imagining myself already in that room, **I wished I could die**. That state would last until the following morning, when the first ray of comfort from the sun, as every day as the gardener resting his ladder against the wall among the nasturtiums which climbed to my window, **would make me jump out of bed and run down into the garden, unperturbed by the thought that some other evening would come when I would once again have to leave my mother**. This was how **I learned from the Guermantes way to discern in myself** **the succession of such moods**, **which at certain times can even divide each day** up between them, **as one of them recurs, displacing the other**, as punctual as bouts of fever; moods which, **though adjacent to each other, are so devoid of means of communication and so foreign to one another that when I am in one of them I am incapable of comprehending,**

> **or even of imagining, anything I may have desired, or feared, or accomplished in the other.**
>
> (Swann's Way, Kindle edition, pp. 184–185)

Answers to the Skiing Exercise

- Skiing for excitement and pleasure (Happy Child)
- Skiing because you must be in shape. (Demanding Parent)
- Skiing to be the best and be admired. (Overcompensator)
- Skiing because of subjugation to your spouse. (Compliant Surrenderer)
- Skiing to escape a spouse who does not like to ski. (Protector-Avoidance)
- Suffering from not performing as well as others on skis. (Vulnerable Child)
- Feeling entitled to go ahead of the others while waiting for the lift. (Impulsive/Undisciplined)
- Yelling at your partner on the way home for being more interested in the other skiers than in you. (Angry Child)
- Disproportionately punishing your child for not following your instructions on the slopes. (Punitive Parent)
- A feeling of harmony between fun and technical mastery. (Healthy Adult)

This Chapter's Main Points

- Schema Therapy (ST) was based on the concept of schemas, but a second concept quickly gained importance in clinical work, that of modes. If the schema is a prediction, the mode describes the response mobilized by the organism when the prediction is activated. This response manifests itself on several levels: physiological, affective, motor, kinesthetic, cognitive, verbal, and so on.
- Clinically speaking, it is easier to have direct access to the answer to the prediction than to the prediction itself, which is most often implicit. That is why we refer to the mode as the first apparent evidence that an issue has been triggered.
- Young originally identified ten modes. Although several other modes were subsequently added, in our opinion they are subcategories of the original modes.

- Each of these ten modes is described in this chapter.
- Since the aim of this book is to revisit ST in the context of the therapeutic reconsolidation process (TRP), we would like to make the following observations:
- The Vulnerable Child and Angry Child modes are fundamental to ST. They indicate that the response to a fundamental psychological need is threatened. These modes are associated with an existential problem and with significant suffering.
- The most primitive solution to suffering is avoidance.
- Dysfunctional strategic modes are the solutions adopted to avoid suffering. These solutions were most often created implicitly in the context of a child's limited resources and were quickly automated. This is what generates the subjective impression that there is no other choice ("I can't help it"). The Compliant-Surrender, Protector-Avoidance and Overcompensator modes are facets of these solutions. We also believe that the Punitive Parent and Demanding Parent modes are often a form of solution, although this may not seem obvious at first glance.
- Finally, any schema transformation based on the TRP involves an update that allows the Happy Child and Healthy Adult modes to occupy more of the person's subjective space.

Notes

1 Quebec and other parts of Canada, France, Morocco, Norway, Switzerland.
2 (2021, p. 98).
3 Detached Protector in (Young et al., 2003).

Chapter 3
Early Maladaptive Schemas as Predictive Memories

We concluded Chapter 1 with our definition of schemas as predictive, primarily implicit, memory organizations, whose function is to promote adaptation by automating as many perception–action modules as possible. Each schema can therefore serve to rapidly assess the resource/threat ratio and trigger the planned solution. In Schema Therapy (ST), the threat is linked to a failure to meet fundamental psychological needs. The solution, on the other hand, reflects strategies for controlling or avoiding the threat, which have become dysfunctional over time.

Our aim is to "revisit" ST from the perspective of a recent paradigm that brings the predictive function of the brain to the fore (Barrett, 2018; Clark, 2023; Hohwy, 2013; Seth, 2021; Solms, 2021). This recent paradigm is essential to understanding what enables the therapeutic reconsolidation process (TRP), that is, the prediction error experience (Ecker et al., 2012, 2024; Ecker & Vaz 2022; Côté & Cousineau, 2022). This predictive dimension is not absent from Young's descriptions of schemas (Young et al., 2003). Our intention will be to put it front and center, to make sure it is explicitly addressed. We will see later, in the chapters on clinical intervention aimed at schema transformation, that it is necessary to precisely define, through discovery work, the specific configuration of the prediction in which the schema is embedded. This level of precision is necessary to enable identification of incompatible living knowledge specific to the prediction (Ecker et al., 2012, 2024; Côté and Cousineau, 2022). In this sense, if you choose to integrate the TRP into your practice with schemas, as is done in Coherence Therapy (CT), **the identification of an early maladaptive schema will constitute a first approximation of the predictions made by the person, and these will need to be refined.**

DOI: 10.4324/9781003628125-4

A good way of finding our way in this process is to understand schemas as predictive systems. The prediction is carried out by means of three questions, which the brain obviously does not ask itself explicitly; we put them into words here to make them clearly understandable. First, the brain will ask itself what the nature of a given stimulus is, based on similar past experiences. Second, the brain will deduce what will happen next based on what has most often occurred in previous experiences. For example, a person with a Punishment[1] schema will become anxious because they anticipate that the other person will get angry and lash out. Third, the brain will draw on similar past experience to determine the best action to take in this context, and immediately activate to prepare this adaptive response. Schemas, which follow this three-beat rhythm, are a way of making sense of other people's reactions and behaviors. Modes, the subject of the previous chapter, are the psychological state in which a person finds themself when a specific schema is reactivated. If it is the Abandonment schema and the person anticipates that the other person is going to let them down, they are likely to experience a sense of panic; this is the Vulnerable Child mode. The reason the individual is in this mode is the prediction made by their Abandonment schema that they will be abandoned and find themself in a state of helplessness. The schemas are the content of the prediction.

Early maladaptive schemas are memories of traumatic or harmful experiences. It is important to remember that there are also adaptive schemas (early and otherwise); one of the aims of therapy is to favor the creation of new adaptive schemas. Early maladaptive schemas are memories with few nuances (extreme generalizations) that trigger automatic, unreflective reactions. These memories correspond to the irrational beliefs listed by Beck and others, because they are usually learned very early and implicitly. They often manifest themselves in a form similar to the form they had at the time of their creation. If we were five years old when we formed this memory, in Vulnerable Child or Angry Child mode, the generalizations and perceptual biases that will be reactivated in the mode will be similar to those of the five-year-old child we were. That is why we will say of an adult who, for example, usually behaves like a wise and eloquent intellectual, but who explodes in anger at a family gathering because someone has moved their plate, that they are reacting like a child. The same applies to a man who sulks for two days because his partner has done something that displeased him. Sulking is associated with a childlike strategy: he expresses his anger by making his partner feel it by sulking, so that they have to guess the reason for his reaction, hoping that the partner will apologize and repair the relationship. This is not a highly sophisticated strategy (this man wastes several hours or even days of his life waiting for his partner to find out what they have done to him, instead of saying it clearly and trying to resolve the problem). It is therefore a primary level strategy.

As we like to repeat, schemas are often reactivated in a form corresponding to the developmental level at which they were created. The individual will have the subjective impression of feeling and behaving like a child of five, six, ten years old. A highly generalized schema (in the family, professional, friendship, academic or marital spheres, etc.) may, however, express itself in more or less varied forms, without systematically bringing forth the full scope of expression it had at the time of its creation in childhood or adolescence. Nevertheless, it will always be possible to recognize the schema's central theme no matter what sphere of life it is expressed in.

Schemas are created throughout our lives, but the schemas identified by Young are mostly created during childhood and adolescence. They concern the fundamental ways in which we function that are developed in the first phase of life. What is more, when a schema is reactivated, it is always in the present moment (recall Edelman's *Remembered Present*, 1989). It is this prediction based on a similarity (it looks like) between what is perceived in the present and what we have experienced in the past, even if we do not have an explicit memory of it. We therefore perceive the present situation with the same degree of threat, fear, panic or anger as when the schema was learned. The advantage of this reactivation in the present is that it gives direct access to the memory when it happens within the psychotherapeutic encounter.

We now present the eighteen early maladaptive schemas defined by Young in his classic textbook (Young et al., 2003). They were originally divided into five domains, each of which constituted a category of impediments to adequate responses to basic psychological needs. As mentioned earlier, we choose to present schemas from the perspective of predictive mental models. Also, we will illustrate our presentations with comments drawn from the experience of one of us (PC) as a practitioner, supervisor, lecturer, and trainer for some thirty years in ST. Our "statistical learning" as to what appeared useful to the therapists we met, in several countries around the world, will form the basis of these comments.

Domain I Themes: Issues of Attachment, Belonging and Acceptance

When the environment's responses to these needs prove inadequate, the person is at high risk of disconnection, shut off from others and rejection. And this will inevitably have an impact on their relationship with themself.

The essential function of attachment for the biological, psychological and social development of the human child is one of the few subjects that are not controversial. Attachment has been studied very thoroughly and now constitutes an imposing theoretical and experimental corpus (Cassidy & Shaver, 2016). The human baby's total dependence on its parents (or any other parental figure) is based on the fact that, without them or the group, it would be doomed to certain death. So, it is hardly surprising that phylogenesis has come to embody this necessity in our primary affective systems.

In a child's reality, how could parents (or other attachment figures) meet his or her needs for connection and acceptance? Ideally,[2] these relationships would offer sufficient

a) Affection: unconditional love at the right moments;
b) Safety: a safe environment with a clear, coherent framework;
c) Stability: an environment that offers a degree of predictability because it is not constantly changing;
d) Support: as their internal and external resources are constantly overwhelmed by what they are experiencing and the situations to which they are exposed, children constantly need help;
e) Protection: children are too small to take care of themselves;
f) Respect: children need their limits to be known and respected, and not abused;
g) Empathy: This is an extremely important need for human beings to feel understood and to see what they experience reflected back to them by another person;
h) Acceptance: Concrete and symbolic survival depends on being accepted by those closest to you, as well as by the group, and this contributes to answering the need for protection;
i) Validation: Children need to feel that they have value in the eyes of others because it is through the eyes of others that they build their identity as they grow up.

As mentioned earlier in this book, our purpose is to integrate the therapeutic reconsolidation process (TRP) into ST. Remember that this necessitates the accurate identification of the predictions that form the underpinnings of a schema in order to pinpoint the kind of living knowledge that could create a prediction error experience, which is a necessary condition to schema transformation. That is why we are going to present each schema in terms of a statement that translates the prediction of that schema (there could be many other statements for each schema).

Abandonment Schema.[3] Given the vital need to connect with others, what is one of the worst possible threats? The breaking or the instability of that connection. Ruptures to connection can come in many forms and to varying degrees. For example, the sulkiness of a parent (temporary rupture), the altered state of a parent who is under the influence of a drug (temporary rupture), the altered state of a severely depressed parent (rupture that can be maintained over a long period of time), the death of a parent (permanent rupture), and so on. The important point to remember about this schema is the notion of a temporary or permanent break in connection.

Predictions about people who are important to us. I can't count on you, nor hope for a stable, resilient connection with you that would provide emotional support and security because you're unstable ... unpredictable ... unreliable ... erratically present ... or, worse, you're going to let me down altogether, abandon me.

We can clearly see the significant impact it has when a person predicts instability in their connections. Even if a connection is intense and strong, there is still the anticipation that it will not continue to be so.

As in all threat-predicting systems, the ratio of resources to threats is fundamental. If, for example, as an adult I am convinced that the person I am in a relationship with is the only external resource available to me in life, the threat of abandonment will be even more lethal.

Mistrust/Abuse Schema. Any threat to our physical integrity obviously has fundamental relevance to our biological survival. One of the gifts of our neocortex is to extend this fundamental concern to threats to the integrity of our self-image. When our self-image is threatened, the organism mobilizes just as intensely as when our physical self is threatened. This is why experiences of threats to our integrity, such as aggression, intimidation, rape, betrayal or humiliation, very often leave deep memory imprints. For our organism, survival is at stake, and very primitive responses (already at the level of the brain stem) are rapidly mobilized: flight, attack, paralysis, playing dead.

Predictions. You will intentionally abuse me … assault me … humiliate me … deceive me … lie to me … manipulate me … humiliate me … seek to take advantage of me.
Trauma level: and there's nothing I can do about it.
In the context of a significant lack of internal and external resources to deal with the threat, a strong sense of helplessness (Vulnerable Child mode) will increase the likelihood of developing post-traumatic stress.

Emotional Deprivation Schema. The Abandonment and Mistrust/Abuse schemas correspond to harsh attacks on connection and personal integrity. The Emotional Deprivation schema is more closely linked to relationship quality. And Young associated it with three fundamental needs:

- The need for affectionate contact, both physical and emotional.
- The need to exist in the eyes of others, to be recognized, heard and understood.
- The need for support, guidance, and protection in the face of challenges that may prove excessive for the child's abilities.

An incomplete response to one of these needs is enough to create the schema.

An Emotional Deprivation schema could be acquired in an otherwise stable, secure family, which sees to the child's instrumental needs such as a good education and concern for material comfort and physical health. In such cases, the Vulnerable Child mode will be experienced as a subjective lack, despite the impression that nothing observable is lacking. Not so long ago, these people would have been described as having neurotic personality structures!

In our opinion, Alice Miller (2008), even though she obviously did not use the term "Emotional Deprivation schema," did refer to the same concept in her famous book *The Drama of the Gifted Child*, while arguing that it is a widespread characteristic among psychotherapists!

Predictions. You won't offer me any warmth or affection ... I'll be left wanting. I can't expect you to understand me, to listen to me, because you have no genuine interest in me. You're not going to provide me with guidance or support in the form of a solid, reassuring presence.

A person can present predictions corresponding to one, two or all three of the types of fundamental needs.

Defectiveness/Shame Schema. This is a schema associated with what is generally referred to as low self esteem. The person considers themself worthless, even despising themself. Unsurprisingly, feelings of shame are regularly associated with this sense of worthlessness. For these people, being seen by others is often a threat, since it means their defectiveness could be unmasked. The level of suffering can be very high when, for example, the person is convinced that they do not deserve to be loved, adding to the feeling of not being loved.

In ST, the Defectiveness schema is usually perceived as the consequence of a lack of validation, criticism or even aggression, on the part of parents or other significant people.

Predictions. If I present myself as I really am (in my true light), I can only be undesirable ... unacceptable ... bad ... repulsive ... unworthy ... in your eyes. It's impossible for me to be loved as I am, for what I am.

In our workshops and clinical work, we now add two further perspectives to the creation and function of the Defectiveness schema. First, the concept of cognitive coherence.

Once language has become part of the human toolbox, another need emerges: the need for cognitive coherence (Cooper, 2007; Grawe, 2007). This is a tertiary-level need. For example, a statement will often provide a justification for an action whose true intention is quite different (Mercier & Sperber, 2017; Wegner, 2002). The young child who acquires language will gradually seek to attribute coherence to everything around them and to what happens to them. Every parent remembers the phase when the child keeps bombarding them with the question "Why?" Here are a few examples of cognitive coherence built around the schemas we have just presented.

- Abandonment schema: No one is there for me, I can't count on anyone being consistently present.
  What does that say about me? I'm not worth it?
- Mistrust/Abuse schema: I can't expect my integrity to be respected.
  What does that say about me? I don't deserve better?
- Emotional Deprivation schema: No one is interested in what concerns me.
  What does that say about me? I am not interesting?
- Emotional Deprivation schema: I don't get any affection.
  What does that say about me? I am not lovable?

If we adopt this perspective, therapeutic work with the Defectiveness schema will be based primarily on interventions concerning the schemas underlying its coherence, rather than directly challenging its content. For example, an adult with a Mistrust/Abuse schema who is able to develop the conviction that their parents behaved improperly with them, that their parents were simply not good parents, will almost certainly modify the conclusion that they deserved such treatment, without it having been necessary to directly address the content of the Defectiveness schema per se.

Finally, the other perspective we consider relevant to the work with Defectiveness schema is that maintaining negative self-talk about oneself may have a strategic function. Ecker et al. (2012, 2024) include low self-esteem in their paradigm of lesser suffering protecting against worse suffering. For example, our adult with a Mistrust/Abuse schema may implicitly prefer to self-attribute responsibility for their parents' abusive behavior ("I didn't deserve any better") rather than face full awareness of the parents' violent or perverse intentionality, because this would simply be unbearable. At the very least, making themself responsible means the person is not totally powerless to change things (they can work on deserving better), whereas the opposite would leave them in a position of intolerable powerlessness. This obviously has a great bearing on therapeutic intervention. Our patient may resist changing their self-talk because of the sense of powerlessness that change would engender.

Social Isolation Schema.[4] Biologist Edward O. Wilson (2015), considered by many to be Darwin's successor, brilliantly argued for a revised theory of natural selection. In addition to selection based on competition between individuals, he put emphasis on selection based on competition between groups. In the latter case, cooperation between group members becomes an immense advantage for the group, and consequently for the individuals making up the group. For Wilson, the importance of group cohesion has played a decisive role in the evolution of the human species, as well as in the growth of its cerebral capacity.[5] If the Abandonment schema corresponds to a direct threat to the need for attachment for individual survival, the Social Isolation schema is its equivalent in terms of the stakes involved in belonging to the group. Both schemas are based on issues of rupture; rupture of attachment and rupture of belonging. So, it comes as no surprise that we observe them so often as major sources of human suffering. In fact, they regularly make media headlines through the tragedies caused by people who were unable to tolerate personal abandonment or rejection by a group.

Predictions about groups outside our family (school, sports, community, work, etc.). You won't accept me, you'll reject me ... you'll ridicule me, ostracize me ... I'll always feel apart, different from others, cut off from the rest of the world ... I'll never feel a real sense of belonging to any group whatsoever.

Comments on Domain I. One of us (PC) has made a habit of pointing out that working with schemas regularly leads us to issues in this first domain. They often make up the foundation of the Schema Map we work with (see Appendix 1 for Figure 5.1 and presentation of Schema Map). Even though, when working with the TRP, we can **never take for granted** that the discovery work will lead us to issues of attachment or belonging (Ecker et al., 2012, 2024), the fact remains that they tend to be extremely commonly encountered (Côté & Cousineau, 2022).

That is why, in our ST workshops (PC), we like to use the typically North American term "Big Four" to refer to the Abandonment, Mistrust/Abuse, Emotional Deprivation and Social Isolation schemas.[6] Our clinical experience (statistical learning) has led us to consider that the more significant these schemas are, the more intense the "worse suffering" will be, and that consequently the strategies to avoid the worse suffering will tend to be more radical (a nervous system in great imbalance tends to mobilize primary-level corrective responses). Think of your clients with borderline personality disorder, often characterized by attachment traumas and chaotic solutions to their worse suffering.

Domain II Themes: Issues of Autonomy, Agency, Actualization and Expansion of Capabilities

When the environment's responses to these needs have proved deficient, the person is at high risk of not being able to rely on their own movement (agency) and personal abilities to take their place as a distinct individual.

If the first human challenge is one of connection, the second is to come to the feeling of being the instigator and actor of one's own choices. Very soon after a child has begun to master language, they start to say "I can do it" (even if it is not really the case). This is the feeling of being at the origin of my own choices and being able to act on them.

Dependence/Incompetence Schema. The opposite of autonomy is dependence, especially the feeling of not having sufficient internal resources to meet the demands of reality, a feeling of powerlessness. This is why people with this schema place great importance on continued access to external resources, which are considered to be better equipped to meet these demands.

Predictions. I'm unable to manage my day-to-day responsibilities, so I absolutely need your help to do so. Without you, I'm screwed, because I'm totally powerless to manage on my own. It's just not possible.

The dependency in the Dependence/Incompetence schema is functional. The much-used expression "emotional dependency" is more of a type of strategy used to cope with Abandonment or Emotional Deprivation schemas. For example, a person clinging insistently to another out of fear of being abandoned.

Enmeshment Schema.[7] This schema is generally learned in a parent–child relationship in which the parent is emotionally just as much in need as the child. The schema manifests itself as an expectation of privileged emotional closeness, unwavering loyalty and the sharing of intimate information (having a secret garden is perceived as a betrayal). The person with this schema does not feel they have an identity of their own (undeveloped self). As the name suggests, they are enmeshed with the other, resonating with what the other is experiencing. This schema can also be replicated in a love or friendship relationship.

You may have noticed that we do not use as such the term "undeveloped self," which is associated with this schema. In our experience, apprentices in ST tend to limit this concept to the Enmeshment schema, whereas undeveloped self is certainly not limited to this schema. Think of Emotional Inhibition, Self-Sacrifice, Subjugation, and so forth.

Predictions. It's impossible for me to distance myself from you because you wouldn't be able to tolerate it. You'd feel abandoned, betrayed by me. It would either destroy you completely or make you so angry. Either way, it would be unbearable for me. Also, I don't think I'd have an identity outside of you, so I'd find myself without direction, in a void.

Failure Schema. Failure schema, like the Defectiveness schema, is linked to a self-image issue, to what I say about myself. While the Defectiveness schema is associated with my value as a human being, the Failure schema is associated with my level of competence, my skills, my ability to function as an autonomous person, as both the source and the actor of my accomplishments. If I have been convinced that accomplishment is impossible or if I cannot achieve something that I think I should be able to achieve, I am likely to have developed the Failure schema.

Predictions in the spheres of school, work, sports, and so forth. I have failed and I will continue to do so. I will be again and again, stupid, inadequate, certainly not as good as all of you. You'll always be dissatisfied with my performance, and that's extremely hard to live with.

Our experience of working on this schema leads us to make the same clarifications as those presented earlier concerning the Defectiveness schema.

In ST, Failure schema is usually seen as the consequence of comments or reactions from parental figures (including teachers or coaches), or from playmates or schoolmates. Comments such as "you'll never do anything right," "you're too stupid," "don't even try, you won't succeed," and so forth.

However, with or without these disparaging comments, the simple necessity of having cognitive coherence will cause the creation of a discourse that makes sense of our experience. For example, "If I haven't developed the sense that I am capable of a certain degree of autonomous functioning, personal competence, individuation: What does that say about me? I'm stupid, inept, not as good as others?"

Here again, the question of the locus of intervention arises. Will the therapist seek to directly challenge the discourse of the FA schema, or will they instead target the experiences that led to its construction? For example, if a parent's expectations, which we were unable to meet, are now experienced as having been excessive, disproportionate, more in line with the parent's needs than ours, then the attribution of the problem is likely to shift from us to that parent. And as a result, without further effort on the part of either therapist or client, the Failure schema will have lost its relevance as a discourse to achieve cognitive coherence.

Finally, as we did for the Defectiveness schema, we recall here the CT point of view (Ecker & Hulley, 2019; Ecker et al., 2024) on negative self-talk, its function being to avoid "worse suffering." Actually, this view is not unique to CT. In ISTDP, for example, self-deprecation is seen as a defense, a way of protecting oneself from an even greater threat (Abbass, 2015; Coughlin, 2017; Frederickson, 2021). Think of your clients who, before broaching a subject with you, warn you that you are sure to find it trivial or unimportant. This is often a way of controlling the situation by ensuring that you will not judge them negatively. Here again, the client will probably show strong resistance to abandoning this strategy, and the associated apparent lack of self-confidence, if the apprehended threat remains unchanged.

Vulnerability Schema.[8] In the sections of this book that concern the use of the TRP with schemas, we will emphasize that the Vulnerability and Negativity/Pessimism schemas cannot be specifically categorized as existential problems with which "worse suffering" is associated, or as solutions to these problems with which "lesser suffering" is associated. This is in line with our impression that these schemas are usually consequences of solutions, or consequences of the absence of solutions.

In its classic version, the Vulnerability schema is defined as an inordinate fear of being struck at any moment by an unpredictable disaster in the following areas: illness, accidents, attacks, loss of emotional control, natural disasters, and the conviction that this disaster cannot be prevented.

Predictions. I'm at the mercy of dangers that can manifest themselves without warning, at any time, such as illness or aggression. Danger can also come from my emotions, which I could lose control over … and who knows what I could do! So, I can't really feel safe, I don't see how it could be any other way.

Of course, several cognitive-behavioral techniques (Beck, 2021) quickly come to mind when we are confronted with such a symptomatic picture, such as cognitive restructuring, exposure, or downward arrow. Acceptance and Commitment Therapy ([ACT]; Hayes et al., 2012) is another interesting option. And we have no doubt about their relevance. We are not calling them into question, we are specifying that we believe they are incremental memory interventions, that is, those techniques aimed at counteracting a memory that has become problematic by creating a new memory. As you will recall, the aim of this book is not to call into question incremental approaches, but to seek a more systematic application of the TRP to schemas. It is also relevant to mention here the subject of working with anxiety which we addressed in our first book (Côté & Cousineau, 2022).

But it is always better to give an example. A patient came to us with a phobia that prevented her from going by herself to shopping malls. However, TRP discovery work led this patient to uncover a fear that had nothing to do with stores or shopping.[9] In fact, this lady was experiencing significant marital dissatisfaction, which eventually manifested in intense feelings of anger that were initially quite foreign to her. It turned out that this anger terrified her because, in her mind, it could jeopardize her marital relationship, a prospect she felt totally helpless about and afraid to face. However, her phobia of big box stores put her in the position of having to rely on her partner for tasks as simple as grocery shopping, which put in check any latent intention towards revolt or autonomy—the real threat to her.

In this example, anxiety has a function. But often, it does not. Take, for example, the fear of becoming a street person or vagrant, which fear, surprisingly, is found in the cases of many people whose social or professional status seems to show not the slightest chance of this happening. In most cases, discovery work will lead us to issues of personal insecurity associated with schemas such as Abandonment or Social Isolation. So-called objective reality (status at work, financial assets, etc.) is simply no match for fears such as being completely isolated, with no one there for us. The need for cognitive coherence will do the rest of the work: If I am experiencing this terrible insecurity, there must be a major danger somewhere! And that can be the start of an obsessive fear.

Whatever the cause, anxiety is a highly unpleasant experience. You will not be surprised, then, to learn that we may seek solutions (avoidance) to this unpleasant experience, even if it does not constitute the basic existential problem that causes suffering. For example, a person may choose to try to lessen the effects of anxiety by drinking alcohol. In our TRP language, a new schema map has just been built on top of the consequences of a first schema map: Ideally, we need to have the patience to go through all the schema maps a person presents because the problems that are really at the root of therapy consultations sometimes have several ramifications, like tentacles on a body.

Domain III Themes: Integration of Limits, Self-Control, Self-Discipline, Recognition of the Existence of Others

Chaos is not conducive to adaptation, either individually or socially. For example, it is hard to achieve one's goals without some form of self-discipline, or it is hard to live in harmony with your social circle if you have no regard for the people around you. Also, the feeling of not being in control, of being at the mercy of our impulses, is highly unpleasant. It robs us of that feeling of personal integration.

Entitlement/Grandiosity Schema. This schema can be acquired in two different ways. First, there is what we would call in everyday language the spoiled child, who is not used to being refused anything. The person with this schema will then generalize this expectation to other relationships: "I want it, so it is owed to me." The other way of creating this schema is in Overcompensator mode. In this mode, a neglected child with a history of inadequate responses to basic psychological needs can develop ways to force the other person to give them what they have not received. "I suffer from not having this, you must provide it." In both cases, the person has developed the conviction that their needs are more important than those of others, that they are entitled to priority treatment, and ultimately that they are superior to others, hence, the term "grandiosity" associated with this schema. It is not uncommon for a person with this schema to become angry, even threatening, if others do not meet their expectations. Also, the person has no empathy for how their actions may make the other person feel.

Predictions. I don't have to follow the same rules as you. I have special rights to which you must respond, or I'll let you know. And I don't have to give you anything in return, nor do I have to worry about you, because I'm in a category of my own, superior to yours.

Insufficient Self-Control/Self-Discipline Schema. Adapted personal and social functioning requires the development of control skills, whether in terms of tolerance to the frustrations of daily life, or the discipline we need to achieve medium- or long-term goals.

It is impossible for everything to work out the way we want it to all the time. People with the Insufficient Self-Control/Self-Discipline schema do not tolerate this fact well. They may display emotional impulsivity in protest of this reality, or their inability to tolerate frustration can manifest in avoidance of anything unpleasant. Integrating frustration or unpleasant emotion is not an option for them.

Many life goals, such as obtaining a university degree, require self-discipline. It would be difficult to get the degree if we were not able to follow a work method over a certain number of years. And, inevitably, there are times when we have to give up pleasant activities (invitations from friends) or we have to do something that we do not spontaneously want to do (such as read a compulsory text that does not really interest us). This self-discipline is often lacking with the Insufficient Self-Control/Self-Discipline schema.

Predictions. I can't stand it when things don't work out the way I want them to. I can't stay with this frustration, it has to come out. Or at the very least, I'm going to find a way to escape this situation, whatever the cost. It's impossible for me to impose regular discipline on myself to achieve a goal that's too far away in time. Depriving myself of immediate pleasures or imposing things on myself that I don't want to do can't last long, it's boring, much too unpleasant.

Domain IV Themes: Inordinate Focus on the Reactions, Needs or Approval of Others

The schemas in this domain have in common an extremely strong preoccupation with other people, whether it is through fear of their reactions, responding to their needs, or seeking their approval. The person with schemas in this domain cannot allow themself to be authentically what they are and fully take into account their fundamental psychological needs without some form of threat showing up. This will obviously have an impact on the person's level of satisfaction since they do not feel that it is legitimate to take into account, express and respond to their own needs. For the most part, these schemas manifest themselves in Compliant Surrenderer mode.

Subjugation Schema. With this schema, the person abdicates to another control over their behavior, decisions and emotional expression. The person thus ignores their own needs, deeming them insufficiently important or valid. This can easily lead to a build-up of frustration and anger, which obviously cannot be expressed openly and directly. The function of this schema is to avoid rejection, punishment or anger by not offending the other person.

Predictions. It's really too dangerous to tell you how I feel or to do anything you don't like. Because if I dare to, you'll either abandon me, or retaliate and punish me. It scares me to death, I panic. The risk is too great.

Self-Sacrifice Schema. Whereas with the Subjugation schema, the threat is mainly external (abandonment, punishment), the threat is mainly internal with the Self-Sacrifice schema, that is, guilt. This is the feeling experienced when the person senses the other's need and fails to meet that need. People with this schema are often at the service of others but do not feel constrained by them; they feel as though the movement towards others' needs comes from within. They can, of course, be easy prey for manipulation (think of a partner with an Entitlement schema). Also, the needs of the person with this Self-Sacrifice schema are often invalidated or minimized.

Predictions. If I don't put your needs before mine, I'm being selfish, and I can't live with that guilt.

In our clinical experience, we have observed that the Self-Sacrifice schema is most often linked to the Emotional Deprivation schema. The following is an overt statement by a client with an ED schema; it was made explicit through discovery work. The client explained that she felt obliged (to avoid guilt) to buy a prom dress for a girl she knew.

> When I see you, X (young girl), not being able to have what at the moment seems essential to your happiness, that ball gown, I absolutely have to go for it. I interpret what you're going through, through my own memories of suffering, which are always painful, like the one when I couldn't go to that week-long vacation class, which seemed like an unhoped-for opportunity to

> experience pure happiness. To lessen this ever-present suffering, I have to make you experience what I was denied. I live it as if there were no other way to deal with my suffering as a little girl, which comes back with a vengeance at times like this, when I'm acutely reminded of what I've missed and what's been done to me.
>
> Source: Author's clinical work

And even if she buys the dress, the hurt will never be fully repaired, and the solution will have to be repeated every time this young girl has another wish.

Approval–Seeking/Recognition–Seeking Schema. It is as if people with an Approval Seeking schema were equipped with a radar to spot anyone who disagrees with what they are saying or doing. The radar is also very good at detecting people who approve, which is what the schema is all about—being approved of. This implies that the schema strategy is to identify what will win that approval from others—the right idea, the right behavior, the right opinion, and so forth. Here too, certain issues linked to the Emotional Deprivation schema come easily to mind. The child is built in the parent's gaze. For many, this quest does not end with childhood—the Approval Seeking schema is a case in point. Approval–Seeking, characterized by a chameleon-like response to the gaze of the other person, is a manifestation of Compliant Surrenderer mode.

However, the Recognition-Seeking component of this schema is often associated with seeking to bait the other's gaze by achieving or possessing socially desirable status or objects, a prestigious professional position, a luxurious car, and so forth. The function of the schema is then one of overcompensation. But unlike the contemptuous "grandiosity" of the Entitlement schema, the Approval Seeking schema manifests itself more as a form of seduction, without the arrogance.

Predictions. It's imperative that I win your approval by saying or doing what you want. It's intolerable for me to displease you, because my personal value is at stake. I have to impress you with my accomplishments or prestigious possessions. It's the only way I can feel like I'm worth something.

Domain V Themes: Little Room for What Is Spontaneous, in Congruence with Our True Fundamental Needs Life Tends to Be Rigid, Leaving Little Space for Pleasure or Authentic Joy

Siegel (2020) likes to point out that the two main categories of mental problems are too much rigidity or too much chaos. In Domain III, we highlighted problems linked to chaotic reactions or behavior. In the present domain, we find ourselves at the opposite pole. Here, control plays a key role. The resulting adaptation may look great (for example, the social success often associated with Unrelenting Standards schema), but it comes at the price of muzzling the Spontaneous Child and its intrinsic vitality.

Emotional Inhibition Schema. When a person uses this strategy a lot, they appear emotionless, rigid and rarely spontaneous. Logical reasoning often plays an important role, leading to rational rather than simply pleasurable choices. In therapy, these individuals have difficulty answering the question, "How do you feel when you talk to me about this?" Emotions clearly represent an internal threat to them, often because allowing themselves to express them heralds an external threat, the critical gaze of the other. This gaze then provokes shame in oneself.

In people who are less constricted and rigid, the schema sometimes appears as a fear of losing control over one's emotions. These people may even be able to express emotion about their fear of losing control.

Predictions. If I allow myself to express my feelings spontaneously, I'll lose control of my emotions and be judged harshly, even contemptuously. I'll feel an unbearable shame. It's too risky … the only option is to keep it all well and truly walled up inside me, and save myself a lot of trouble.

Unrelenting Standards Schema.[10] With this schema, there is a strong internal pressure to meet high performance targets and to follow rules to the letter. Also, energy must be expended efficiently, without wasting time on things that are considered unimportant. This pressure is self-generated, even if the original source may have been external.

This schema is most often seen in Overcompensator mode: securing a position that cannot be criticized, for example, by ensuring that you have an answer to everything (perfectionism). In this case, it is not the SEEKING system that drives the intention to know "everything," but rather the FEAR system aimed at ensuring protection against attacks (criticism). From the outside, the result might appear similar, but the subjective experience will be very different: the relief felt after each successful counter-attack, that must be repeated with each threat, is very different from the true pleasure and satisfaction of learning, of knowing.

The Unrelenting Standards schema can also present itself in the Demanding Parent mode. In these cases, the aim is not to overcompensate for a vulnerability that could be criticized, but rather to maintain a response to parental demands (or other parental figures) that have become part of oneself. The continued use of this capitulation strategy most often has a function of which the person is unaware (implicit learning), and which they are not yet ready to let go of.

Predictions. I have to do everything perfectly, I have to have total mastery of the subjects I'm working on, I have to be in complete control of everything I do. That's the only way I can avoid being taken to task and criticized. Because I absolutely can't bear to be seen to be at fault, the sensation is unbearable … I lose all my bearings, my world collapses.

Punishment Schema. The Punishment schema has two positions, one when we are being punished, the other when we are punishing. In the first position, we are in a Child mode, in the second, in Punitive Parent or Overcompensator mode. We will explain in Chapter 5 why we prefer to work with the first position and, consequently, use the term Punishment schema rather than the original term, Punitiveness schema (Young et al., 2003).

In Vulnerable Child mode, the Punishment schema most often manifests itself in the FEAR system. We are terrorized by the person (or mode) punishing us. The education value of the punishment, if there is one, is thus fused with a disproportionate emotional intensity not conducive to appropriate learning. If the punishment is violent, we are right at the edge of the Mistrust/Abuse schema. However, with the Punishment schema, even if the punishment is excessive, the person knows why they are being punished. Individuals with a Punishment schema easily become terrorized when they perceive the sky turning stormy in relationships, their sense of powerlessness being easily triggered.

We consider Punishment schema in Vulnerable Child mode to be one of the existential problems linked to basic psychological needs (Chapter 5). As with the Mistrust/Abuse schema, the need for protection has not been answered by a parental figure. Also, a parent has frequently been the source of the punishment. Often, the Punishment schema will be accompanied by another schema whose function is to avoid this "worse suffering." The Subjugation schema is an excellent example: not opposing in order to avoid punishment.

In Punitive Parent mode, the person occupies the position of the aggressor. They become intolerant of certain people (especially those close to them), not accepting the slightest deviation from what is expected. Often, the person themself does not escape this punitive intolerance: the slightest deviation is not tolerated, and is punished.

Predictions. If you get angry with me because I've done or said something you don't like, I'll be terrorized, paralyzed, with no way of defending myself.

Negativity/Pessimism Schema. In our introduction to the Vulnerability schema, we presented our point of view on the Negativity/Pessimism schema. Its position in the Schema Map (worse suffering—solution—lesser suffering) may vary, and should therefore be the subject of discovery work. Our clinical experience consistently confirms that this schema can hardly exist on its own. These gloomy predictions about the future often have to do with the level of attachment security. A secure attachment would not lead to the prediction that one day you will find yourself in a situation where everything is collapsing and you find yourself totally helpless.

The fact remains, however, that this schema presents itself in a characteristic form: predicting that there is a very high risk of things going wrong, that when things go wrong it will bring us major problems, and that we must therefore always be vigilant and on our guard. Preventing these predicted catastrophes can take up a lot of space. Obsessive-compulsive rituals are a good example.

Regarding intervention, the Negativity/Pessimism schema poses the same question as the Vulnerability schema. Do we try to tackle these convictions directly, or do we try to understand their coherence before anything else? This is the question that is at the heart of this book. The answers are to come. In its classic version, the Negativity/Pessimism schema may look like the following predictions.

Predictions. Things are bound to go wrong, to deteriorate, whether it's losses, mistakes with serious consequences, betrayals, and so on. So

I have to remain extremely vigilant and on the lookout for the slightest hint of deterioration, so that I can focus on everything I can do to prevent catastrophe.

Conclusion

We have just presented Young's schema model from the perspective of its predictive function. Our early maladaptive schemas are constructed from our experiences by statistical or rapid learning. The question now is what we can do therapeutically with these predictions. What can we do to reduce their power over our lives (manage them), or to radically change them (modify or transform them)? The following chapters answer this question more thoroughly.

This Chapter's Main Points

- In this chapter, our aim is to revisit early maladaptive schemas from the perspective of a recent neuroscientific paradigm which emphasizes the predictive function of the brain.
- This predictive dimension was not absent from Young's descriptions of schemas. Our intention is to bring it to the fore, to make it more explicit.
- From the perspective of the therapeutic reconsolidation process (TRP), the transformation of a schema requires an experience that is incompatible with our prediction, the experience of a prediction error. Making a prediction explicit increases the chances that the brain will realize what is incompatible with it.
- The schemas identified by Young are general categories of human experiences; they refer to our common humanity. That is why they are so easy to relate to. **However, the TRP teaches us that for an element of reality to be truly experienced as incompatible with our prediction, it must be perfectly calibrated to the specificity of that prediction.** In this sense, the identification of a schema constitutes a first approximation of the predictions made by the person, which will need to be refined. This is what we will see in the chapters that follow.
- Nevertheless, schemas provide important reference points for the main types of predictions. If, metaphorically speaking, the specificity of a prediction corresponds to a branch of a tree, or even a leaf, the schema would be the tree itself.

- As explained in the previous chapter on Child modes, the schemas identified by Young are created during childhood and adolescence. They are therefore mostly related to issues of attachment and belonging. As Ecker regularly points out though (Ecker et al., 2024; see Chapter 5), other schemas can be created in relation to distinct issues.
- This chapter contains the definition in predictive format of each of the eighteen early maladaptive schemas.

Notes

1 Later on, when we define this schema, we will explain why we use Punishment instead of Punitiveness as in Young et al., 2003.
2 At the same time, Winnicott's comment on the "good enough mother" (or other caretaker [Winnicott, 2005]) should be remembered as a way of tempering inordinate expectations. In this book, we use "good enough parent."
3 Abandonment/Instability (Young)
4 Social Isolation/Alienation (Young)
5 Living in a group requires a high degree of proximity between individuals, each of whom may represent a threat or a resource for the others. Hence the importance of developing acuity in assessing the intentions of others ("mind reading"), an acuity that has required an increase of the frontal cortex.
6 We could possibly add a fifth when the Punishment schema is extreme and approaches abuse.
7 Enmeshment/Undeveloped Self (Young)
8 Vulnerability to Harm or Illness (Young)
9 We've learned not to be surprised anymore.
10 Unrelenting Standards/Hypercritical–ness (Young)

Part II

Facilitating Transformational Change in Schema Therapy

Chapter 4
Schema Intervention—To Manage or To Transform

Schema Therapy (ST) has already established its efficacy as a treatment approach. Roediger et al. (2018) and Brockman et al. (2023), provide overviews of the relevant research.

Moreover, as Ecker & Vaz (2022) point out, the question of the type of change achieved has important implications for psychotherapy. To our knowledge, this question is rarely addressed directly in ST (this is also the case with many other approaches). We believe that it would benefit from being addressed directly, and it is precisely this issue that has led us to write this book.

It has already been pointed out (Ecker et al., 2012, 2024; Côté and Cousineau, 2022) that the difference between an intervention leading to incremental change, that is, new learning aimed at neutralizing the target learning, and an intervention whose mechanism of action is the therapeutic reconsolidation process (TRP) rests on three elements that are essential components of the TRP:

- Reactivation of learning target (the schema whose transformation we aim to achieve).
- Experience that is contradictory to the learning target (a mismatch triggering a prediction error).
- Juxtaposition of target learning (the schema as the initial emotional truth) and an experience that is contradictory to this prediction (both cannot be true at the same time). Repetition of this juxtaposition enables the learning target to be erased and rewritten by new emotional learning.

DOI: 10.4324/9781003628125-6

In our opinion, many ST interventions already include ingredients that can be used to increase the probability of bringing about the transformation of problematic models of reality in a more deliberate way. That is why it is a good idea to be familiar with the TRP steps to foster this type of change.

In this chapter, our aim is to highlight the difference between **managing** and **transforming** schemas. We will do so by exploring two techniques used in ST:

1. One of the authors of this book developed the Mindfulness Flash Card (Cousineau, 2012; Cousineau & Ngô, 2013). This type of intervention philosophy (contextual approach) is also the basis of the book by Roediger et al. (2018).
2. In his 2021 book, Remco van der Wijngaart formalized an experiential technique that has defined the work of many schema therapists since Jeffrey Young created the approach. The name of this technique is "imagery rescripting."

We think it is worth pointing out the difference between the types of learning that can occur in therapy, and highlighting the ingredients needed for genuine emotional memory transformation, if that is the goal we are aiming for. Incremental change and transformative change have very different impacts on the brain (Ecker & Vaz, 2022), and both have empirical validation for their respective and mutually exclusive effects. With this distinction in mind, the choice is entirely yours. Our mission is simply to provide you with the best means of making an informed choice.

Mindfulness Flash Card (MFC)[1]

Tara Bennett-Goleman (2001) was the first to propose the use of mindfulness with Young's early maladaptive schemas. It turned out that this way of working had a certain family resemblance to an approach that was beginning to make its mark in psychotherapy at the same time, Acceptance and Commitment Therapy ([ACT]; Hayes et al., 1999, 2012).

It was in the same spirit that the MFC was created. The idea was to diminish the power that schemas exert over a person, to help the person be less at the mercy of their schemas; a way to help change the typical assertion "I can't help it." At the time, we described the technique as a way of managing schemas. In today's vocabulary, we might add that it is an incremental learning process that can have a regulating effect on the schema but does not transform it.

Step 1: Learning a Mindfulness Technique. The first step of the intervention involves the person learning a mindfulness technique. It is aimed above all at creating greater tolerance to the somatic experiential component of the schema, the one that drives us to do something to end the unpleasant experience. For example, using alcohol to neutralize feelings of sadness or anger, or acting impulsively to release tension. This technique obviously requires input from the tertiary brain level. The following paragraph describes this step.

I feel now, in the present moment. Instructions: I simply stay with what I feel in my body (somatic sensations, affects, action tendencies) for a few minutes. I observe what I feel without trying to change anything. If what I feel changes, I simply stay with this new sensation. I am not judging what is happening, and I don't follow my thoughts; when a thought pops up, I notice its presence (I may say "a thought") and I come back to what I feel. The philosophy behind this exercise is "What is, is" (I fully realize that my schema has been triggered).

Learning to "live with" rather than "react to" becomes a regulatory tool (internal resource). The target learning (the schema) is not rewritten but mastered.

Step 2: Mentalization. The affective regulation of step 1 favors a more effective use of cognitive resources, including those that enable mentalization through the mode and schema model in MFC step 2. If you recall our exercise on the Abandonment schema in Chapter 2 (p. 30), the lady in the scenario could have realized that her schema had been reactivated and that it echoed her personal history more than the current situation she was faced with. The concepts of modes and schemas help to make explicit a reaction that, at the outset, is largely implicit and experienced as an emotional truth. Once made explicit, schemas can be experienced differently, such as "It's my schema that leads me to predict that." Here again, the schema is not rewritten; mentalization acts as an internal resource.

Steps 3 and 4: Understanding and Acting as a Healthy Adult. Following steps 1 and 2, the person is in a better position to act from the Healthy Adult mode, favoring an understanding and response that ensure that their fundamental needs are taken into consideration with a focus on long-term benefits rather than immediate relief (step 3: Sound Judgment). For example, is compulsively checking my partner's mobile phone best for the long-term quality of our relationship? Finally, step 4 of the MFC, called Just Action, involves acting on this sound judgment in Healthy Adult mode. As ACT practitioners point out (Harris, 2007), while it is difficult, if not impossible, to choose how to think or feel, it is possible to control our behaviors and align them with our sound judgment (in coherence with our values).

It is worth noting that the development of all these internal resources (mindfulness, mentalization, sound judgment, just action) takes place through the therapist's intervention, which in this context constitutes an external resource for the patient. The patient will now be better equipped to deal with their schema; they will be less at its mercy. The use of the MFC becomes a tool to put the brakes on a pure and simple reactivation of the schema that would have otherwise led to undesired states or consequences.

More often than not, however, the schema maintains its predictive conviction, which is modulated by the learned technique. Of course, the more this newly acquired memory can be reinforced by regular practice, the more likely it is to enable resisting the schema (target learning). On the other hand, certain contexts may nevertheless reactivate the schema: a particularly emotionally charged situation, the abandonment of the technique learned in therapy (the MFC in this case), fatigue, hormonal changes, illness, and so forth.

So, what might enable us to move from incremental learning, that keeps the schema under control without transforming it, to unlearning the schema? Aiming for conditions that can enable the TRP to be applied. The MFC, particularly in steps 1 and 2, already contains components that can be used towards this goal.

The simple recognition that a schema has been reactivated, without judgment or opposition, satisfies the need to understand why our reaction is actually coherent. A prediction (implicit semantic memory) has been activated, and the person is convinced that they recognize a situation and know how it will unfold, as if nothing has changed since the schema was created.

Here, we refer to our Internal/External Resources/Threats Matrix. If nothing had changed since the schema was created, this would mean that the person has the same resources and faces the same threats at, say, thirty years of age, as they did at, say, six years of age. It is understandably tempting for a therapist to confront this belief directly using cognitive techniques. However, according to our understanding, this would be more likely to create incremental learning than to favor a process of unlearning. Therefore, we seek to create an experience of prediction error instead.

Thus, the predictions implicit in the Abandonment schema, in our example from Chapter 2 (p. 30), could be based on this lady's apprehension of being in intolerable distress if she were abandoned by her partner (prediction of insufficient internal resources), or on the convisction that, since no one else could be interested in her, it would be impossible to find another partner (prediction of the unavailability of other external resources). As for the prediction concerning external threats, it could be the anticipation that the spouse would behave exactly as an inconsistent parent did.

We can see, then, that there are several potential gateways to a shift in the predictions made according to the target learning, the Abandonment schema in this case. If we were to ask the patient to make an open-ended statement based on her predictions, it might look something like this:

> X (her partner), you're just like Dad, who has let me down so often, so I can't trust you. As he did, you're going to abandon me and that will be absolutely intolerable for me, I'll never get over it. And no one else will ever take an interest in me and become a reliable companion. Nothing has changed, I'm still the fragile, helpless six-year-old girl at the mercy of your instability. It's unbearable suffering.
>
> Source: Authors' clinical work

In our training courses on Coherence Therapy (CT), we have observed that this type of overt statement is surprising to therapists at first sight. Yet, encouraging the patient to fully immerse themselves in their emotional truth (integration), rather than opposing it, is a crucial step in the TRP. In this sense, steps 1 and 2 of the MFC favor this integration by having the client recognize and immerse themself in the reactivated schema. The concomitant use of the mindfulness technique ensures that the level of activation remains within a tolerable zone, another essential condition for new learning. And self-compassion, another element that favors integration, usually follows the mindfulness exercise.

Let us return now to the lady's open statement to her companion (to be used in imagery, not in reality), which is associated with experiences with the woman's father. A first possible mismatch could be time-based: this is the reactivation of a memory built up many years ago. Saying this explicitly can provoke the sudden conscious realization that there is a difference between the current situation and the memory being reactivated. Indeed, an exercise used in CT, "I am in memory" (Ecker et al., 2012, 2024; Côté & Cousineau, 2022) is aimed directly at creating this kind of mismatch experience, namely the realization of being under the illusion of fully reliving a situation from the past that is no longer relevant in the present context, a realization made possible by the explicit perception of the temporal dimension that enables juxtaposition. In this example, we can see that all it took was a few adjustments to mobilize simultaneous conscious attention to the explicit prediction of the schema and to the characteristics of the situation taking place in the here and now.

The statement in our example also presents other possible sources of mismatches in the predictions of the matrix quadrants:

1. Internal resources: "Intolerable for me, I'll never get over it," or "I'm still the fragile, helpless six-year-old at the mercy of your instability."
2. External resources: "No one else will ever take an interest in me and become a reliable companion."
3. External threat: "You're just like Daddy."
4. Internal threat: "It's unbearable suffering."

For each of these predictions, there is potentially an incompatible piece of knowledge already present in the person's memory. If this is not the case, various therapy interventions can serve to help the person recognize an incompatible piece of information or create one (see Côté & Cousineau, 2022). And when incompatible knowledge allows us to experience prediction errors (TRP step 2), and rewrite the schema (TRP step 3), we can integrate the incompatible information into our original formulation of the MFC. For example, this could become, "This is exactly the type of situation (spouse's late arrival) that made me say I was in serious danger because I'm still the fragile, helpless six-year-old at the mercy of your instability, but I know now that this is no longer true. I'm no longer that fragile, helpless little girl, but a grown-up woman with the resources to cope with life's situations, even those that would cause me great distress. X, I still want to live with you, but I no longer feel at your mercy; I simply want us to be happy together, each doing our part."

So, we can see how knowledge of the TRP can add value to the techniques we already use. Directing our attention to the dimensions of reactivated predictions (schemas) and potential prediction errors, promotes schema transformation rather than creating incremental learning that keeps the schema under control without changing it.

Imagery Rescripting

Young (2003) has consistently emphasized the relevance of therapeutic work with experiential techniques, particularly mental imagery techniques. van der Wijngaart (2021)[2] has dedicated an entire book to imagery rescripting, in which he mentions adapting his protocol from the work of Arntz and Van Genderen (2020). This therapeutic technique, first described by Smucker et al. (1995), offers an opportunity to engage the TRP, even unbeknownst to those who have been applying the technique for all these years. Let's not forget that, since TRP is an innate and natural mechanism for all nervous systems, it can be triggered in both single- and double-blind conditions. We are going to suggest a number of adjustments that can be made to make the most of this opportunity and enable you to use it in a systematic and targeted way, if you wish to do so.

Let us begin by tracing some of the steps in the protocol proposed by van der Wijngaart. To do this, we will follow an example of a patient he uses in his book, "Nicky," who is upset following an argument with her boyfriend (the situation brought to the therapy session). The therapist does not ask the patient to describe the situation, but rather to re-experience it through mental imagery, which obviously helps to reactivate the memory (the target learning).

Nicky. Before exploring the recent situation and its associations with the past, and sensing a certain reluctance on the part of the patient, the therapist chooses to carry out an exercise in which the patient imagines a safe place that can be retrieved, should the emotional intensity become too high. It is a technique designed to ensure that the level of activation remains within a tolerable zone—a condition, we remind you, essential to all steps of the TRP.

Comments. Using a safe place is a new experience that can build new learning. This technique therefore adds to the patient's internal resources. In our comments, we will systematically come back to the fact that this learning could be incremental or transformative. If it is incremental, it will serve to combat avoidance of the problematic issue: the patient could have been saying that things have gotten better and that she does not really want to revisit the situation. However, the learning could be transformative if it combines the steps of the TRP. For example, the tendency to want to avoid the issue could be an implicit strategy based on the prediction that it would be too painful, intolerable, to work on the issue. In Nicky's case, the use of the safe place (internal resource) and the support of the therapist (external resource) lead her to successfully pursue the exercise. Guiding her to consciously identify her prediction (it'll be too painful, I won't be able to do it), and on the realization that she is actually able to complete the exercise (fostering a possible prediction error experience), enables the juxtaposition step of the TRP to take place, leading to genuine transformation. This is one of van der Wijngaart's objectives: "If you were afraid of the ferocity of your emotions, the treatment will help you to be less afraid of allowing those emotions in" (p. 264).

Let us go back to the next step of the imagery work.

Nicky. The therapist guides an exploration of the recent marital conflict. The patient relives this situation, in which her boyfriend is very angry with her and calls her stupid and imbecile. The therapist asks her how she feels when she is told this (situation always played out in the present moment—memory always reactivated). She replies that it's horrible, that she feels "awful, sad, scared and guilty ... that it's all my fault" (p. 75). This puts her in Punitive Parent mode ("all my fault").

The therapist then moves on to the next step of his intervention and introduces the affective bridge to the past technique. He asks the patient to stay in touch with how she feels in the situation where she is the victim of her boyfriend's anger, and to let associations from the past present themselves spontaneously. Nicky then finds herself in a scene when she was five years old, in which her father is extremely angry with her as he revisits a situation in which she spilled juice in the car: her father's face is flushed and he yells at her (external threat). Taking into account the level of activation raised in the patient (internal threat), the therapist chooses to join her in the mental imagery scene (external resource), and will have her return to her safe place afterwards (internal resource). This allows the patient to regain a tolerable level of activation, and answer her need for safety. The therapist then returns to the exercise, explaining the coherence of her reactions (learning history) and the father still inside her, criticizing her and telling her she's done something wrong (Punitive Parent mode).

Comments. In ST, it is traditional to seek to clarify the link between current schema activation and childhood experiences. As already explained at the start of this book, working with the Vulnerable Child and Angry Child modes is of great importance in ST, as it enables us to revisit the person's relationship with their fundamental psychological needs. van der Wijngaart adds: "With imagery rescripting, we'll change how you view the terrible events that have happened to you. We can't erase the memories, we just can't, but we'll help you to get a different sense of what happened and to experience it so strongly that it changes the meaning of the events" (p. 264). This can be translated into the language of CT (Ecker et al., 2012, 2024; Côté & Cousineau, 2022) as: "You can't really change episodic memory, but you can change implicit semantic memory." Therefore, imagery rescripting serves this objective. Here again, the question arises as to the type of change that will occur: Will it be incremental or transformative? Rescripting of childhood scenes in imagery certainly has the advantage of reactivating the target learning (the schema) on which we are seeking to intervene. In our model, this means that the predictions of our Resources/Threats Matrix will be in play. Now, this patient's (Nicky's) predictions were based on the perceptions of a five-year-old girl with no real external resources to help her cope with difficult situations. The question now is how to deal with these predictions. We will look at this in the next part of the therapeutic intervention.

It is important to mention that in CT, work on the predictions of our implicit semantic memory does not always require work on the episodic memories at the source of these predictions; what is necessary is an experience of prediction error.

We have now come to the active phases of therapeutic intervention through imagery rescripting. Roughly speaking, they take place in two steps.

Nicky. First, the therapist intervenes in the childhood scene in which Nicky is severely reprimanded by her father. Later, the patient will draw on her own Healthy Adult mode to rewrite this childhood scene with her father. The therapist ensures that this is experienced at both somatic and affective levels, an important concern when seeking to intervene on memories. This is always done with the patient's full agreement, and progressively to respect her processing rate.

In ST, we consider that reactivating the Child modes risks bringing back the same feeling of powerlessness in which the patient found herself at that moment. Hence the therapist's decision to intervene initially in the imagery scene. The protocol calls for the safe place to be used at the beginning and end of the exercise, as well as if the patient deems it necessary. In the exercise, little Nicky finds herself with her angry father. She's very frightened, feeling that she's done something wrong (Vulnerable Child mode). It's at this point that the therapist enters the picture and steps in between father and daughter. Then he confronts the father outright: "I want you to stop hurting Nicky and talking to her like that! I won't allow it. I decide what happens now, we decide what happens now, not you! I'm not scared of you. What's wrong with you, treating your little girl like that?" (p. 102). The therapist then asks the patient how she feels. She says she feels a little safer, now that she's not alone in the situation. The therapist continues to intervene in the situation. At the end of the exercise, the patient says she now feels safe.

Comments. If the patient now feels safe, something clinically interesting has happened. But what exactly? Is it a one-off experience of relief, a learning experience linked to a specific context (the therapy), or a transformative experience? It is hard to say at the moment. In ST, we consider that we have taken care of "little Nicky". We took her fear into account (empathy), we defended her (protection). But did this change her predictions about the availability of external resources more generally? Or, could the therapist's reassurance have created a reaction in the patient to the effect that she could also defend herself and that this would be entirely legitimate, or even that it was the father's behavior that was incorrect, not hers? Could the answer be all of the above? Impossible to say, at first glance. So, how could we find out, and potentiate a possible discrepancy with the patient's predictions? Simply by asking her what happened **in her experience** during the exercise. This could take the form of: "What makes you feel safer now?" If, for example, she were to answer, as one of our patients once did, "This is the first time in my life that someone has taken my side, defended me," then there would be a juxtaposition between her prediction made explicit (no one ever takes my side) and this new experience that someone has taken her side. Indeed, Nicky gives a clue to her experience when, in response to the question about how she feels now, she says that she feels safer because there's now someone with her.

As we can see, increasing the chances of an experience being truly transformative may require only minor adjustments to our intervention. In this example, what exactly has happened in the patient's experience? No intervention in psychotherapy has a perfectly predictable impact; each person is a subjective universe in their own right. So, it's worth checking what has happened in the experience of the person we're working with.

Nicky. Following this interaction in imagery between the therapist and the father, and the patient's calmed state, the therapist proposes a relaxing imagery exercise in which he suggests that she imagine the two of them in a garden where the patient is enjoying herself under her therapist's compassionate gaze.

We are sure you understand by now that new internal resources can be either incremental learnings that will add tools to oppose schemas, or sources of mismatches to predictions of resource insufficiencies that can lead to transformative changes.

In the next phase of imagery rescripting, the therapist will focus on building the patient's internal resources, working first to strengthen her Healthy Adult mode. It is with this mode that the patient will then confront her father in a rescripting that will then rely on her own resources. Note that van der Wijngaart (2021) provides important clarifications on the use of this technique, depending on the nature of the patient's difficulties[3] (post-traumatic stress, severe personality disorders, etc.); it is important to be aware of these if you choose to intervene in this way.

The therapist first explains to Nicky why it is important to reinforce her Healthy Adult mode; psychoeducation is another characteristic facet of ST. He then gives a personal example of his own use of his Healthy Adult mode in a situation with his teenage daughter. In this way, he uses himself as a model for his patient. Not only does he do this through verbal description, he also adds his experience of "explicit awareness" of the emotional, cognitive, physiological and postural facets of his Healthy Adult mode. Experiential psychoeducation can serve as a contradictory experience. Here again, it would be interesting to explore the subjective experience that this intervention created for the patient, to assess whether its impact could actualize the steps of the TRP.

In the next step, the therapist asks the patient to recall a difficult situation that she was able to cope with, a manifestation of her Healthy Adult mode. Nicky describes a job interview she handled well, despite her nervousness and fear (internal resources enabling her to cope with her Vulnerable Child mode). Then, as he did in his personal example, the therapist asks her to pay attention to different facets of the state she is in (feeling "good, strong" [p. 147]) and to repeat this exercise between now and the next session.

It is now Nicky's Healthy Adult who will gradually respond to the needs of the Child (internal resources). The therapist ensures that the experience of the Healthy adult is embodied in physical sensations (felt sense). We are now ready to move on to helping the patient gain greater autonomy in caring for and protecting her Vulnerable Child. The therapist first reactivates the memory of the Vulnerable Child who was the victim of her father's excessive anger because she spilled her juice in the car. But this time, he does not intervene in the imagery. Instead, he coaches the patient to reactivate her Healthy Adult mode and bring it into the situation. The aim is for this mode to defend little Nicky against her father, and to show compassion for her.

In the rescripting exercise where Nicky confronts her father, as the therapist did earlier, the therapist makes suggestions and validates the steps she takes (external resource). Once the patient has succeeded in getting her father to leave the room where he had come to remind her of the car incident, she takes over the task of comforting little Nicky, who has just witnessed the scene. At the end of the scene, big Nicky feels good and little Nicky is delighted.

The last step of this intervention is very interesting from the perspective developed in this book. To put it metaphorically, we would say that we are on the doorstep of the TRP. This is a rescripting exercise in which there will be experiential interaction between Nicky in Vulnerable Child mode and Nicky in Healthy Adult mode. van der Wijngaart describes the objectives: "the rescripting from the perspective of the healthy adult will strengthen a feeling of strength and self-confidence: 'I can do something!' Experiencing the rescripting from the perspective of the child/victim touches on the need to be seen, to matter: 'Someone's standing up for me. I'm being taken care of!'" (pp. 161–162).

Little Nicky is delighted and reassured by the experience. Interestingly, the author mentions that it is not necessary to return to the safe place (a transformation has occurred?) Also, in the feedback on the experience, the therapist asks the following questions: "What have you learned? … How did it feel to stand up for yourself like that? … Where did you feel that? Can you still feel that a little bit?" (p. 279). And he concludes by suggesting using written or audio flashcards extracted from the session.

Comments. Many of the proposed exercises are designed to counter the Punishment schema[4] in the Vulnerable Child mode. They therefore will likely create incremental learning to counteract the position of vulnerability. This is already a therapeutic success. Also, as we have already mentioned, the TRP may occur in a double-blind fashion, outside the conscious intentionality of both patient and therapist. Moreover, this dialogue between little Nicky (Vulnerable Child mode) and big Nicky (Healthy Adult mode) is akin to an experience of juxtaposition. In fact, a juxtaposition could very well occur spontaneously as a result of the dialogue, or of listening to the session again, and so on. Or, we could add to our chances by intentionally increasing the likelihood of a prediction error experience happening. For example, by getting the patient to fully inhabit her two alternating modes: I'm alone, scared and powerless, and I'm now strong enough to defend myself. These are two incompatible positions that it would be useful to maintain in the field of conscious attention at the same time. The "victim" position could then simply disappear once and for all, with no effort required to maintain this transformation (the result of the TRP).

Before concluding this exploration of the imagery rescripting intervention in ST, we would like to address another issue linked to our experience with CT—that of the function of the symptom. In Nicky's example, she feels guilty, and that she has done something wrong. The therapist's intervention is aimed at directly opposing this description of herself, challenging it. Yet, through discovery work in CT (Ecker et al., 2012, 2024; Côté & Cousineau, 2022), we often discover that feeling like a bad person has a function for the person. For example, in the case of our patient who lived with a mother who wouldn't accept the slightest remark or reproach without attacking her daughter verbally and physically. Our patient quickly understood, implicitly, that the only way to ensure a certain relationship with her mother and avoid aggression was to systematically attribute all blame to herself. Avoiding her mother's rage and rejection was a matter of survival. In this context, seeking to modify the Punitive Parent mode would require taking into account its survival function, with all the predictions that this entails.

This Chapter's Main Points

- This chapter focuses on the nature of the changes achieved as a result of psychotherapeutic intervention. We recall the distinction between incremental change, aimed at neutralizing a target memory through new learning, and transformative change, based on the therapeutic reconsolidation process (TRP), aimed at annulling the target memory and rewriting it through new emotional learning.
- In our opinion, many Schema Therapy (ST) interventions already include ingredients that can be used to increase the likelihood of bringing about the transformation of problematic models of reality in a more deliberate way. That is why it is a good idea to be familiar with the steps of TRP to foster this type of change:
    - Reactivation of target learning (the schema whose transformation we aim to achieve).
    - Experience that is contradictory to the learning target (a mismatch triggering a prediction error).
    - Juxtaposition of target learning (the schema as the initial emotional truth) and an experience that is contradictory to this prediction (both cannot be true at the same time). Repetition of this juxtaposition enables the learning target to be annulled and rewritten by new emotional learning.
- Incremental, or counteractive change, is about **managing** a schema, while transformative change is about **changing** it. We think it is worth pointing out the difference between these types of learning that can occur in therapy, and highlighting the ingredients needed for true emotional memory transformation, if that is what you are aiming for. Incremental change and transformative change have very different impacts on the brain, and both have empirical validation for their respective and mutually exclusive effects. With this distinction in mind, the choice is entirely yours. Our mission is simply to provide you with the best means of making an informed choice.
- Based on two therapeutic procedures used in ST, we illustrate the dimensions to which it is advantageous to pay particular attention, and the interventions where we can take them into account if we wish to promote the TRP. These therapeutic procedures are:
    - Mindfulness Flash Card.
    - Imagery rescripting.

Notes

1 The complete Mindfulness Flash Card can be found in Appendix 2 on page 147.
2 All quotations in this chapter are taken from van der Wijngaart, R. (2021). *Imagery Rescripting: Theory and Practice*. UK: Pavilion Publishing and Media, Kindle Edition.
3 Schema Therapy was one of the pioneering interventions to help patients with severe personality disorders.
4 (See our position on this schema in Chapter 3, p. 69)

Chapter 5
Schemas and the Therapeutic Reconsolidation Process–Conditions Required for Schema Transformation

We are now starting a chapter that we hope will be as exciting for you as it is for us. It is time to introduce you to a working method that enables the transformation of emotional schemas, that is, to destabilize and rewrite schemas directly in the semantic memory. To find out more about the neuro-bio-psychological mechanisms involved in this process, we invite you to consult Ecker et al. (2012, 2024), which deal with the subject in depth.

The main thing to remember is this: Schemas are learned and constructed through experience, and they are unlearned and rewritten through experience. The necessary experiences are called "contradictory experiences" or "incongruent experiences," because they precisely infirm the predictions made by the schema.

To transform a schema, we need to create experiences that will enable the person to discover **the emotional truths that explain the need to produce the symptoms that are the schema's "signature"** in everyday life (and which are usually the reason for consultation). Once the person has taken agency by becoming aware of the function of the symptoms in terms of the emotional truths and recognized how this plays out in their functioning, two scenarios are possible. In about half the cases (based on the personal experience of various therapists, including our own), contradictory living knowledge is already available in memory, and will tend to pop up in the person's field of attention as their schema becomes explicit and integrated. This happens when the mismatch detection system, always on duty because our survival depends on it, perceives an incongruence between the schema's prediction and the reality perceived at the same time in conscious experience. It is as if the schema's activation sends a sonar wave into the field of attention and memory and

DOI: 10.4324/9781003628125-7

triggers a revealing "beep!", drawing the person's attention to the mismatch. All that is needed then is to focus on this mismatch, in a neutral but very targeted way, to name it, and to experience it a few times, so that the schema is then rewritten in a new form (Ecker et al., 2012, 2024; Côté & Cousineau, 2022). The rest of the time, it will be up to the therapist to guide an experience in which the discrepancy between what the schema predicts and, what the contradictory experience strikingly shows, can lead to a mismatch detection experience. The schema will thus be destabilized, and a few repetitions of these experiences in the following minutes will suffice to bring about its rewriting (transformation). Examples will be given in the following sections.

It is important to bear in mind that the intervention will be adapted according to whether or not the individual has had traumatic experiences, even though the mechanism of action remains exactly the same (the therapeutic reconsolidation process [TRP]). A clarification on intervention with traumatic memories can be found in Chapter 6 while discussing intervention on the internal threat of the Abandonment schema. We will start with the method for intervening with implicit semantic memory, which is the one most often referred to when talking about schemas.

There is nothing more radically effective to bring down a building than to destabilize its foundation, its base. The same principle applies perfectly to schemas, but to achieve this destabilization, we need start by conceptualizing schemas into two broad categories. At the foundation level, we find schemas that predict significant suffering: Emotional Deprivation, Abandonment, Mistrust/Abuse, Social Isolation and Punishment schemas. In the other category, we find schemas whose main function is to put into action some form of solution aimed at avoiding or limiting the worse suffering, predicted by foundation schemas: these are Unrelenting Standards, Subjugation, Self-Sacrifice, Approval Seeking, Entitlement, Emotional Inhibition, Dependence, Enmeshment, and Insufficient Self-Control/Self-Discipline.

We consider four schemas to be special cases in terms of these two broad categories. The Defectiveness and Failure schemas are at the crossroads between a prediction of significant suffering and a solution aimed at avoiding even greater suffering. Vulnerability and Negativity/Pessimism, on the other hand, are the consequences of the solutions or the lack of solutions to apprehended suffering. We are fully aware that we may at times depart from the original Schema Therapy (ST) model. We do so with a view to systematically applying TRP to schema work. Of course, this leaves you entirely free to position yourself in one paradigm or the other, depending on the type of change you are seeking for your clients.

When the aim is to transform schemas, you will first guide the person through experiences in which they come into contact with the emotional truths that contain the predictions of worse suffering, as well as the rules surrounding it (existential problem). We will look at examples of each schema that might fall into this category. You will also accompany the person through experiences that will enable them to come into contact with the emotional truths that explain the need to adopt certain strategies to avoid this worse suffering (solution).

Each time an important element of discovery is made, you will then assist the person in integrating, immersing themself in and viscerally recognizing these emotional truths in their psychological landscape. A very simple technique called "overt statement" in Coherence Therapy ([CT]; Ecker et al., 2012, 2024; Ecker & Hulley, 2019; Côté & Cousineau, 2022) consists of affirming these emotional truths out loud, with full sincerity, and addressing them emotionally and poignantly to the people concerned (in imagery), as in a cry from the heart.

Once the specific details of the schema have been made explicit, and the person fully and naturally recognizes their presence in his or her functioning, you can move on to the transformation step.

Let us see how this applies, schema by schema. We will be using the Schema Map as presented in our 2022 book (Figure 5.1. For a detailed explanation of the Schema Map, see Appendix 1). At the root of each Schema Map is an existential problem. To help you discover all the relevant facets of the existential problem, we have divided this part of the map into four sections representing the Resources/Threats Matrix as perceived by the schema, and thus reflecting the dilemmas and problems relevant to the context surrounding the schema's creation.

Note that each section of the Resources/Threats Matrix combines with the other sections to group together the different facets of the schema; some facets may be more predominant or central than others in a given schema; this is to be assessed for each schema, with each individual. The only category that inevitably appears in all schemas is the "internal threat," of which worse suffering is always a part. In cases where a schema predicts that internal states may trigger violent behavior in another, for example, this state also becomes an internal threat. These categories are memory aids; we invite you to consult them simply to help you pinpoint predictions that may still be implicit and draw a more accurate or complete picture of the existential problem. This is particularly important when it comes to transforming the schema. As we will see later in this chapter, the places where the schema is clearly out of step with reality vary from schema to schema, and from person to person.

We will therefore present each schema in terms of emotional truths organized within an existential problem predicting a worse suffering. Please note that as each emotional memory is unique, the examples we give represent only themes commonly encountered in psychotherapy; the list will be far from exhaustive enough to encompass the totality of human possibilities! Also, please note that the emotional truths we are about to list, depending on how they are expressed, could sometimes reflect resources, sometimes a form of threat. The important thing, in the end, is to be able to grasp the essence of an existential problem (which makes the presented symptom necessary to produce; this is pro-symptom, or even pro-schema coherence!).

Please allow us one last clarification before we begin the description of schemas as predictive emotional truths. ST has made an **extraordinary**

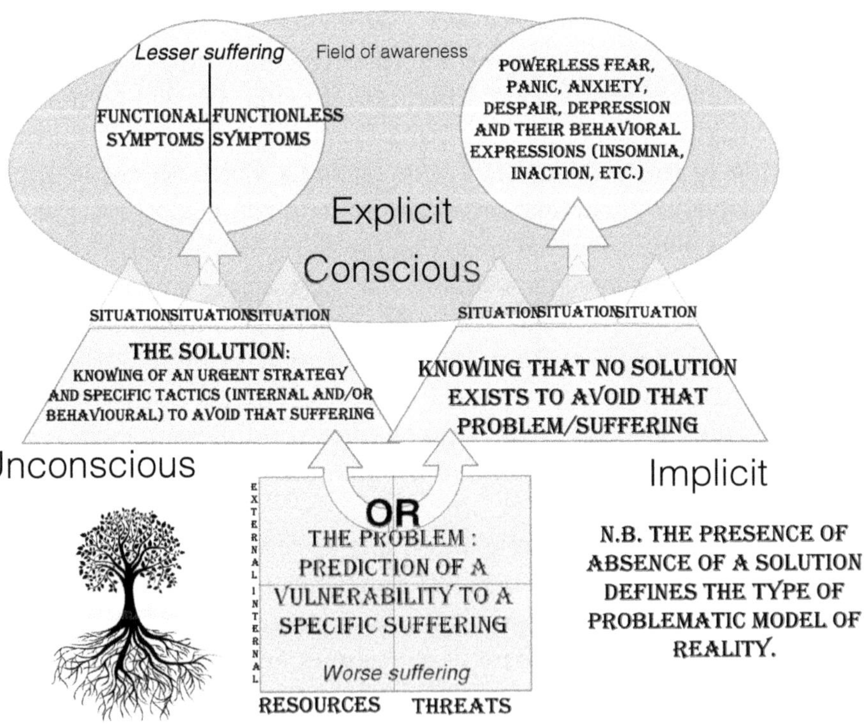

Figure 5.1 Schema Map

contribution to the clarification of the way in which human beings perceive reality. Without necessarily knowing it consciously at the outset, the schema approach fits almost effortlessly into recent paradigms of brain function as a predictive module (Barrett, 2018; Clark, 2023; Hohwy, 2013; Seth, 2021; Solms, 2021). Obviously, it is impossible for a set of concepts to cover the full scope and complexity of these predictions. However, a conceptual model, to remain useful, must offer us points of reference to guide our action. If we were to account for all the specificities of all individuals, the list of schemas and modes would be infinite. We propose an intermediate model. We believe that the basic model presented by (Young et al., 2003) provides a sufficient foundation for effective clinical work. But this base can be enriched in two ways: either by adding schemas and modes, making the model increasingly complex without ever making it exhaustive, or, working from the basic model and integrating the tools offered by CT to enrich each schema and mode with the specificity of the learning of each individual. For example, no two people with an Abandonment schema have absolutely identical experiences associated with the schema. CT discovery work (Ecker et al., 2012, 2024; Ecker & Hulley, 2019; Côté & Cousineau, 2022) aims to clarify what is specific to the experience of a given schema for the person with whom we are carrying out this exploration. At this point, you are probably predicting that we prefer the second option and will be sharing it with you in the rest of this book.

Section 1. Schemas Linked to Existential Problems

Abandonment Schema

- "Nothing has changed, I'm still as fragile and vulnerable as ever, unable to function on my own emotionally, unable to give my life meaning without you."
- "At any moment, I can experience a rupture in our relationship, our emotional connection; everyone ends up abandoning me in one way or another."
- "I am incapable of being alone, even during a short absence, because my distress is unbearable!"
- "No one else is going to be interested in me; you're my only chance at a relationship."

- "I can't count on you or hope for a stable, solid connection with you."
- "You're incapable of providing me with emotional support and security because you're unstable and unpredictable, unreliable, erratically present."
- "If you abandon me, I'll be destroyed, overwhelmed by such intense distress and panic that I could kill myself. I'm going to feel so alone!"
- "If someone is better than me, I'll lose my place in your heart and you'll lose interest in me."
- "Any change in mood or sign of distance in you means you're abandoning me."
- "If I don't live up to your expectations, our emotional bond will disappear; if I'm myself, you won't stay with me (being myself is dangerous)."

Let us illustrate the **four quadrants** of our **Resources/Threats Matrix** with the following examples. The prediction that others are incapable of offering a stable relationship is mainly linked to rules relating to **external resources**, while the prediction of not being able to tolerate a moment's absence would reflect a rule about the person's **internal resources**. Similarly, a prediction that an experience of disappointment in another person will lead to an act of abandonment makes that disappointment an **external threat**, while the experience of despair and loneliness during situations of abandonment represents the worse suffering, which is always a form of **internal threat** that the individual will seek to avoid.

Mistrust/Abuse Schema

- "Nothing's changed: I'm still as small and vulnerable as ever, unable to stand up or run away when you ..."
- "The pleasure I've felt from abuse means I've seduced ..., and knowing this, I'm incapable of looking after myself, making good choices, trusting myself, and so on."
- "At any moment, you can turn against me and do me harm; I lose your protection, your support, and so forth."
- "No one is here to protect me from your attacks."

- "Dad/Mom remains impassive/impotent when you explode."
- "If I report my attacker, no one will take me seriously."
- "If you get angry, I'll become overwhelmed with unbearable terror and helplessness and feel as if I'm going to die."
- "If you assault me, I'll feel soiled again and so ashamed."
- "If you humiliate me, I'll feel like a nobody."
- "You're all looking to take advantage of me, just like (original abusive person)."
- "If I'm not hypervigilant, you're going to hurt me intentionally, just like (original abusive person)."
- "You're all like (original abusive person); if you're nice to me, it's to use me."
- "You'll all end up betraying me, because you're all (liars, manipulators, disloyal, dishonest, etc.) like (original abusive person); there's always something fishy going on, no one is trustworthy in life."
- "In life, you're either the one in control, or you're the one who's crushed; so goes power."
- "You've all mistreated me in one way or another all my life and if I don't do something about it, it will go unpunished/passed over in silence, and it's unacceptable to have to live with this rage!"

Let us illustrate the **four quadrants** of our **Resources/Threats Matrix** with the following examples. A prediction that those who are supposed to offer protection will do nothing to prevent or stop abuse illustrates an **external resources** problem, while predictions anticipating powerlessness or an inability to protect oneself against dangers illustrate an **internal resources** problem. Similarly, a prediction about the rules surrounding the onset and course of abuse concerns **external threats**, while the anticipation of the physical or emotional suffering caused by violence (or the re-experiencing of suffering caused by a given trigger) comes under **internal threats**.

Emotional Deprivation Schema

- "Everyone is like (unfit attachment figure)."
- "You won't really be there for me."
- "I won't interest you."

- "You won't understand me and you won't try to."
- "You can't help me when I need advice."
- "You won't show me the affection or attention I need."
- "The love, appreciation and compassion I feel for myself are not enough to satisfy my need."
- "I don't have the right to exist with my needs, my desires, and so forth."
- "Even being surrounded by people who love me, I will continue to feel that it is insufficient to fill my horribly suffering void."
- "It's unbearable to think that no one on this earth can fulfill my needs so that I can stop feeling my emotional void."
- "Every time I think I've found THE person of my dreams, I'm inevitably disappointed."

Let us illustrate the **four quadrants** of our **Resources/Threats Matrix** with the following examples. A prediction that no one will be available to give attention, presence, support, and so forth, illustrates an **external resources** problem, while predictions anticipating the inability to be content with self-compassion concern **internal resources**. Similarly, a prediction of unbearable emptiness and loneliness concerns **internal threats**, while the anticipation of a reaction of emotional coldness or emotional disharmony in an attachment figure comes under **external threats**.

Social Isolation Schema

- "I'm so different from others that it's practically impossible to be part of a group; every time I try, it'll fall through, and no one will understand me."
- "In the presence of others, I'll feel like an alien, and that's an unbearable experience."
- "I don't have the social skills to be accepted by a group, and I'll systematically find myself on the outside."
- "If I try to fit in with a group, I'll be rejected, humiliated and laughed at; I'll feel so small, ridiculous, alone and ashamed."
- "I'm convinced that my death would go unnoticed."

Let us illustrate the **four quadrants** of our **Resources/Threats Matrix** with the following examples. A prediction describing the impossibility of finding a place in a group illustrates an **external resources** problem, while predictions anticipating a deficiency in social skills concern **internal resources**. Similarly, a prediction of rejection, intimidation or humiliation concerns **external threats**, while the anticipation of a feeling of exclusion, loneliness or shame is associated with **internal threats**.

Punishment Schema

In Chapter 3, we pointed out that this schema appears in Vulnerable Child mode when we are the victim of punishment. On the other hand, if we are the punisher, we are in Punitive Parent or Overcompensator mode. In our Schema Map, the existential problem associated with the worse suffering lies at the base; in the case of the Punishment schema, the feeling of terror and powerlessness is in the internal threat quadrant. This is why, in this section on existential problem schemas, we prefer the term Punishment to Punitiveness. In our model, Punitiveness would refer to a form of solution (e.g., being the aggressor rather than the aggressed).

- "If I dare to claim the slightest right to having my needs taken into account, you're going to attack me and that terrifies me."
- "If I dare displease you, Mom, you'll attack me, and if I dare try to defend myself, you'll try to kill me, and that terrifies me."
- "At the slightest mistake or misstep, you'll put me down and then I'll be completely crushed and ashamed."
- "Nothing's changed, I'm still as weak and vulnerable as ever when you get angry with me."
- 'If I don't make every effort to succeed, you'll cut off all support."
- "If I hurt you or show you my pain, you won't be able to stand being so upset, you'll resent me and stop talking to me for days."
- "Mom, when you lose it and make a scene, as long as I don't take the blame, you'll go days or even years without talking to me."

- "If I let you convince me that I'm valuable, it will invalidate Dad's opinion; he'll explode with anger, destroy me, and my whole family will abandon me because if they don't he'll abandon them too."

> Let us illustrate the **four quadrants** of our **Resources/Threats Matrix** with the following examples. A prediction of cut-off access to support illustrates an **external resources** problem, while predictions describing significant weakness and vulnerability to punishment concern **internal resources**. Similarly, an emotional truth describing the triggers that would make the person believe a punishment is imminent is in the realm of **external threats**, while the anticipation of an experience of terror, shame or powerlessness accompanying the experience of punishment is in the realm of **internal threats**.

Section 2. Special Cases (in Terms of the Schema Map)

In our metaphor of the building we wish to bring down (transforming a schema by making it lose its emotional realness), we emphasized that the most radically effective way to do this is to destabilize the building's foundation. In our model, it is the schema that predicts major suffering that constitutes the foundation. We have just presented these schemas in section 1. The category of schemas to come in section 3 is made up of those schemas whose main function is to put into action some form of solution aimed at avoiding or limiting the experience of the worse suffering.

There is also a group of schemas that are special cases in terms of this distinction. These are the Defectiveness and Failure schemas, which we cover in this section, and the Vulnerability and Negativity/Pessimism schemas, which we discuss in section 4.

In Schema Therapy (ST), the Defectiveness and Failure schemas cover image-related issues, that is, self-esteem (Defectiveness) and self-confidence (Failure). Why do we call them special cases? Because, depending on the perspective from which we are working, they can be both predictions of major suffering and ways of putting into action a form of solution aimed at avoiding or limiting the experience of even greater suffering. This implies that, in our Schema Map, depending on the schema we are working on, these schemas will sometimes be solutions and sometimes they will be the existential problem at the base of the map. In our metaphor, they will sometimes be the foundation of a building, sometimes the roof of another building which you might discover by exploring the basement of the first building (or even by opening a large, mysterious cupboard …).

Example. Consider the case of the person who was the victim of denigration by a parent during childhood, adolescence and probably still is today. She comes to you, as we often hear when meeting a new client, because she wants to improve her "self-esteem problem." When you create experiences that allow this person to get in touch with the emotional truths that prop up their Defectiveness schema, you discover something like this:

> I'm still convinced that Mom is right: I must prove that I'm the best and capable of achieving perfection on the first try to deserve the acceptance and love of others. It's still the only way I can have value. So even though it's causing me a lot of anxiety, I'm going to keep on proving my worth.
>
> Source: Authors' clinical work

This client's experience of mismatch detection, as described at the start of this chapter, was to immediately come up against contradictory knowledge already present in her explicit memory at the time of integrating her schema (Unrelenting Standards to avoid the suffering associated with the Defectiveness schema). This contradictory knowledge: her boss had just given her a very positive performance appraisal, despite the fact that she had been forced to take on fewer tasks than her colleagues to avoid burnout. But the transformation didn't happen. Why didn't it? Two discovery sessions later, this other building appeared, right next to the previous one:

> When you have a spectacular crisis and overreact, I have to be the one to repair the relationship by taking the blame on myself (even if you're the one in the wrong) and putting myself down and denying my opinions and values; otherwise you'll never make

the first move, and you'll go days or even years without talking to me. I'm willing to go through this for the next 30 years, to keep some semblance of a relationship with you.

Source: Authors' clinical work

As you can see, if this client allows her Defectiveness schema to be transformed by her contradictory experiences and knowledge, she will be exposing herself to abandonment. By keeping the constructs of her Defectiveness schema alive and active, she avoids exposing herself to even greater suffering,[1] the devastating loneliness of abandonment.

Now that you have these images in mind, let us see what kinds of emotional truths you will typically find in these schemas. As you may have guessed, in our paradigm for transforming schemas, we would encourage you to always explore the basement to find the door to the next house. In CT, as in AEDP[2], ISTDP[3] and other transformative therapies, self-deprecating talk that feeds low self-esteem and self-confidence is always seen as a strategy for avoiding even worse suffering (Ecker et al., 2012, 2024; Fosha, 2021; Frederickson, 2021). In ST, the Flagellating Overcontroller mode (Brockman et al., 2023; Edwards, 2022; Simpson, 2020) has a similar function. It is a strategy (coping mode) that aims to prevent attacks or punishment, reduce the risk of humiliation, and protect the family from disintegration and its consequences for the individual.

Defectiveness Schema

- "If I share my secret garden with you and you react with boredom/anger/disgust/rejection/condescension, I'll feel an unbearable shame and feel that I've lost all value in your eyes."
- "If I present myself as I am, you'll put me down and reject me."
- "I'm contemptible/unacceptable; if you don't like me, you'll reject or attack me."
- If I let myself be myself and experiment, I'll still experience rejection, shame, feel inadequate and punished for just being myself, that I don't belong, that I bother others and am only tolerated.
- "If I reveal my vulnerability/my flaws/my faults, you'll leave and I'll lose you. I will lose the value I have for you and the little love I am able to feel from you."
- "Even though I have people who make me feel important and like I have value and a place, I refuse to integrate it, because it's the only

way to protect myself from losing everything when you're going to abandon me like everyone else."

- "No one important to me could respect or value me, no matter how hard I tried."
- "I'm convinced that it's impossible to have any real value in your eyes; if you appreciate me, it's because you're wrong about me (or it's out of pity for me, or it's just to please me)."
- "By valuing myself, I'll stop trying so hard to be loved, and everyone will abandon me."
- "If my parents have never been able to love me enough, it's because there's something unacceptable about me."
- "If I let anything convince me that I'm worthy and deserving of respect and consideration, you're going to get even angrier and attack me."

Let us illustrate the **four quadrants** of our **Resources/Threats Matrix** with the following examples. A prediction announcing abandonment or rejection caused by an unveiling of imperfections concerns an **external resources** issue, while convictions about low fundamental value are linked to **internal resources**. Similarly, any emotional truth describing the triggers predicting a form of abandonment, exclusion or attack is in the domain of **external threats**, while the anticipation of an unbearable experience of shame comes under **internal threats**.

Failure Schema

- "If I'm incapable of succeeding in an intellectual field, it means I'm good for nothing, because truly intelligent people should succeed in all intellectual fields."
- "I'm so convinced that I'm going to fail (and feel like such a loser), that it's not even worth trying."
- "Everyone's better than me; I'm a failure."
- "If I don't perform as well as others, that means I'm a loser, and others will succeed in life and I won't; I'll become a drag on others and be pushed aside, and then I'll relive the shame I experienced when I was a loser in Dad's eyes."

- "I'll never be chosen among the first in team sports, and that hurts me deeply."
- "I'm convinced that you all see me as a loser; if you congratulate me, it's out of pity or politeness."
- "My failures or inadequacies trigger an unbearable sense of humiliation."
- "Everyone does better than me, and it's so uncomfortable to be around them!"
- "When I succeed, it's because those who could surpass me are incapacitated or absent. My successes, when they exist, have no real value."

> Let us illustrate the **four quadrants** of our **Resources/Threats Matrix** with the following examples. A prediction of abandonment or rejection due to poor performance or failure describes an **external resource** problem, while beliefs about the inability to perform are linked to **internal resources**. Similarly, all situations involving a risk of failure fall into the domain of **external threats**, while the anticipation of unbearable discomfort, humiliation or shame from a fiasco belongs to **internal threats**.

Section 3. Schemas Linked to Solutions

We are now entering a category of schemas that primarily represent a solution aimed at avoiding contact with suffering (see the previous two sections). As these solutions are imperfect, they entail costs; the costs are the price to pay for avoiding even worse suffering (the Social Isolation schema, for example), they are called "lesser suffering" in CT (Ecker et al., 2012, 2024; Ecker & Hulley, 2019; Côté & Cousineau, 2022). They therefore reflect the agency of the person who makes an (implicit) choice between two sufferings. The box in the previous sections therefore no longer applies, since the solutions aim to avoid contact with the elements of the Resources/Threats Matrix. In the Schema Map, the schemas of the current section are found at the level of the arrow above the Matrix (see Figure 5.1), where the solutions are indicated.

Unrelenting Standards Schema

This schema reflects the mobilization of internal and external resources to achieve various forms of performance.

- "The only way I can interest you is to dazzle you with my knowledge."
- "There are two possible positions in life: perfect/competent or lousy; I have to be the best at everything I do and always look my best."
- "To be good, I have to have thought of everything and understand everything."
- "My biggest fear is that there'll be a flaw in my logic or my knowledge and I'll still look like an idiot, even though I'm a director. And then I'll feel like being with my mother again, so everything that comes out of my mouth has to be perfectly worked out and not open to criticism."
- "I absolutely need people I admire above me to push me to become better and remedy my mediocrity and low self-worth; I always have to put pressure on myself to perform; otherwise I'll let myself go."
- "Everything has to be perfectly organized and in order; otherwise I feel anxious."
- "I must never settle for anything less than perfection, even if it means never feeling good enough or satisfied."

The central theme of the Unrelenting Standards solution, in Overcompensator mode: excel/control to avoid being punished, abandoned, humiliated, devalued, excluded, ashamed, alone.

Note that in ST, when the Unrelenting Standards schema manifests itself in the Demanding Parent mode, it no longer has the function of counter-attacking to avoid the suffering described above. Instead, the emotional truths expressed in this mode reflect a pure reproduction of the rules of attachment as learned integrally through contact with attachment figures. The classic intervention in ST is to oppose the attitude of the parents at the source of this schema. To promote a transformation of this schema, we need to take into account the framework dictated by the TRP. In this sense, we should seek to discover the function of maintaining the Unrelenting Standards schema—in other words, we should seek to discover in what way is it a solution for the person. Those kinds of issues are already addressed in the work of Simpson (2020) and Edwards (2022) in ST.

Subjugation Schema

- "Everyone's like Mom: If you're not comfortable in the relationship anymore, you'll leave; it's my responsibility to do everything I can to make sure you're comfortable and happy. If you're not, it's my fault, and the only way to have a bond with you is to take care of you and especially Mom, even if it makes me very anxious."
- "If I let you down, I'll lose your love and that will destroy me. It terrifies me, and it's as unbearable as when I was a child, to live this terror. I have to avoid this at all costs by always making the right decisions to avoid displeasing you."
- "If I don't let you do what you want, the consequences will be terrible!"
- "If I do what I want, it's going to create serious problems, reprisals, rejection, and so I absolutely must submit to your wishes and desires, let you have the upper hand over me."
- "Even if it means I no longer know my own needs and desires, I still have to let you choose for me, even when it comes to the important decisions in my life."
- "If I don't take the burden of your anguish on my shoulders, you will, like my parents, find me unbearable and stop loving me, or reject me. So, even if it's an immense burden and stress for me, I mustn't give myself the right to be myself."
- "I have to do everything I can to please you, otherwise you'll reject me."
- "I'll do anything to avoid a confrontation, even if it means tolerating the intolerable."

The central theme of the Subjugation schema solution, in Compliant Surrenderer mode: disregarding my needs, opinions, and preferences to avoid being abandoned or provoking irritation and anger in the other person.

Self-Sacrifice Schema

- "Your needs take precedence over mine; if I don't meet them, my guilt will quickly become unbearable."

- "If I prioritize myself in my needs, I'll automatically become the selfish monster I don't want to be, thinking of myself above others, lacking empathy, becoming blinded by my navel-gazing."
- "I must always be careful never to be above anyone else, making others my absolute priority and making every effort to be the one who never abandons them and protects them to the end, even if it means wearing myself out."
- "It's very wrong to let others down, to refuse to help them or to disappoint them; I'll always find time for others."
- "It doesn't matter if I give more than I receive, I know how to make do with little anyway, because my needs are minimal."
- "It's normal to devote myself without receiving any gratitude; I can never give you enough."
- "It's absolutely necessary to take care of the people I'm close to; otherwise it's like abandoning them or treating them with indifference, and that would be wrong."
- "When you really love someone, you accept them as they are and there's nothing my love couldn't tolerate or endure."
- "I couldn't be happy knowing that those I love are unhappy or in need; that would be appalling egocentricity!"
- "You can always count on me to listen to your problems, I'll never abandon you!"

The central theme of the Self-Sacrifice schema solution, in Compliant Surrenderer mode: always put other people's needs before my own, otherwise I'll feel guilty, selfish.

Approval Seeking Schema

- "I can only have a relationship with you if I totally meet your expectations and don't cause you any disappointment or frustration. If the opposite happens, you'll reject me and I won't be part of your group anymore; that terrifies me!"
- "If I let you down, I'll lose your love and that will destroy me. It terrifies me, and it's as unbearable as when I was a child, to live this terror. I have to avoid it at all costs by always making the right decisions to avoid displeasing you. Every time I disappoint you, I panic, and the only way to find relief, like when I was little, is to beat myself over the head."

- "I want everyone to love me, even those I don't like!"
- "It's my fundamental responsibility that no one in the world should have regrets about me. That's why, whenever I risk hurting your feelings, I have to do whatever it takes to resolve or avoid conflicts, even if it means always putting myself last and living under enormous pressure on a daily basis. If I refuse this responsibility, I'll hurt your feelings, and that guilt would be unbearable for me."
- "I have to choose my actions according to what will please you the most."
- "I have to adapt to your expectations."
- "My value depends on the quality of my network and the people who give me attention."
- "It's not worth the effort if no one recognizes it."
- "My choices must take into account your opinion of them."
- "It's unbearable not to have the attention of others!"
- "The only way to feel valuable is by having your appreciation, and I need that almost every day."

The central theme of the solution in the Approval Seeking schema, in Compliant Surrenderer mode: Always behave in such a way as to exist positively in the eyes of others and attract positive attention from them.

Entitlement Schema

- "The only way I can be satisfied is if you match my emotional needs perfectly, at all times."
- "I expect you to keep my frustrations to a minimum; everything in our lives should always be quick and simple."
- "It's still unbearable that you refuse to meet my needs; I demand that you change your ways!"
- "I deserve to have special permissions in life; it's normal for someone like me to be able to bend the rules."
- "My needs are the most important; I can only consider yours if mine are met first."
- "It makes me angry not to have what I want; I have to find a way to control this situation!"
- "No one has the right to tell me what to do!"

The central theme of the Entitlement schema solution, in Overcompensator mode: always seek to fulfill my needs first, in order to escape the frustration of waiting or having to give up, anticipated as unbearable and/or unfair.

Dependence Schema

This schema is based first and foremost on a prediction about internal resources. The individual is convinced of being unable to survive or simply function without the contribution of external resources, which are perceived as absolutely essential. Anything that might cut off access to external resources becomes a de facto threat (whether internal or external).

- "If you're not there, I won't make it."
- "I'll never be able to manage life on my own because I'm so incompetent, I feel so overwhelmed."
- "It's much too big for me to do without you; I absolutely need you."
- "Only you know how to take good care of me."
- "I'm incompetent in most areas of my life; I need you to help me every step of the way, or I'll never make it."
- "My judgment is so unreliable that I absolutely need you to validate my decisions."
- "Nothing's changed: I'm still as vulnerable and irresponsible as a child; I absolutely need you to tell me what to do every day."

The central theme of the Dependence schema solution: I have to rely on you to function on a daily basis, because that is the only way I can overcome my powerlessness/incompetence.

Enmeshment Schema

- "It's my duty to always stay close to my parents, so I can protect our very close relationship; otherwise I'll make them suffer and that would be unbearable."
- "If I allow myself to be myself, my parents will feel betrayed; I have to avoid being anything that might make me too different from them."

- "My mother, my father, my partner, couldn't survive without my closeness to them."
- "It's good to be an open book with Mom; it's bad to have a secret garden; I have to confide in her every detail."
- "My mother is my best friend; I absolutely must prioritize our relationship above all others to keep it that way."
- "I must be one with my partner; it's the only way to know true, strong love."

The central theme of the Enmeshment schema solution: ensuring unwavering emotional closeness at all costs to avoid the guilt of betrayal or the threat of loss of identity.

Emotional Inhibition Schema

- "It's so painful to be in perpetual anxiety of being rejected by others and having to live by countless rigid rules to escape it, that I prefer to stay at home in my inner world and not leave it."
- "If I let myself be myself and experiment, I'll still experience rejection, shame, feeling inappropriate and punished for just being who I am, that I don't have my place, my reason for being, that I bother others and I'm just tolerated, just like at school. It would be so painful, I have to avoid it at all costs by cutting myself off even more from what I feel and am and preventing myself from experiencing what I feel or desire, and being spontaneously myself."
- "I absolutely have to stay in control of myself, in word and deed."
- "My anger is dangerous; we have to do everything we can to stop it coming out and hurting you!"
- "I have to restrain myself from expressing my emotions, even my positive ones, because things can go terribly wrong and then I'll be overcome with shame and regret!"
- "I mustn't let myself express my spontaneity or warmth."
- "I always have to remain impassive in all circumstances."

The central theme of the Emotional Inhibition schema solution: exercising continuous control over the expression of emotions and spontaneous impulses, to avoid criticism, shame and loss of control.

Insufficient Self-Control/Self-Discipline Schema

- "Part of me is convinced that the only way to deal with my stress is to drink/eat/consume, and so forth (in limbic language, we avoid formulations that depict clients as the victims of their symptoms)."
- "Even though I know they have to be done eventually, it's so boring to do the tasks that I prefer to put them off for as long as possible."
- "I hate to make you sad, but I must let you know how I feel, even if it means speaking without filters or restraint."
- "It's out of the question for me to sacrifice my pleasure to meet the demands of a project."
- "It's so hard for me not to achieve my goals that I prefer to give up on them."
- "The only way to calm my anger is to tell you what I really think, right now!"
- "It's best not to push myself on a difficult task."
- "Part of me is convinced that it's best not to force myself to do things I don't like to do, even if another part of me knows it's to my detriment."
- "Even if it hurts my relationships, I have to be transparent and authentic; that's the most important thing!"

The central theme of the Insufficient Self-Control/Self-Discipline solution: giving in to the pressure of primary systems to avoid anticipated suffering related to obeying rules, meeting a deadline, giving in to the requests of a person or project, or emotional and behavioral inhibition.

Section 4. Schemas Linked to Costs

As mentioned at the beginning of section 3 of this chapter, solutions learned in the context of the original development of a schema, or in the contexts of its generalization, are not perfect. They often reflect the makeshift means that were available when the person was a child or teenager. As life becomes more complex, the costs of the solutions also tend to rise, often prompting the person to seek help. The Negativity/Pessimism and Vulnerability schemas are often the consequence of operating with various schemas that deprive the individual of a sense of security, cut them off from vitality, lead to various problems and conflicts, or exhaustion. They are also a reflection of the individual's highly skewed perception of people and situations, which is consistent with the context in which the perception was constructed.

Vulnerability Schema

Vulnerability is a schema that reflects a perception of oneself as being highly exposed to various forms of suffering. This perception may lie at the root of the schema (perception of self, world and others as threatening) or at the level of the consequences of operating with another schema (e.g., a solution such as Unrelenting Standards may lead the individual to feel constantly at risk of failure, which in turn would expose them to humiliation, rejection, abandonment, etc.).

- "I constantly feel that something terrible is about to happen."
- "Life is unpredictable, and at any moment a financial, natural or personal disaster could happen to me."
- "At any moment, I could be attacked or fall ill."
- "The pressure I feel all the time is driving me crazy!"
- "At any moment, my stress can overwhelm me and make me panic."
- "The world is a very dangerous place where I'm not safe."

Negativity/Pessimism Schema

- "Happiness doesn't last; something always comes along to destroy it."
- "When something good happens, something bad always follows."
- "I'm convinced that whatever I do, I'm going to end up penniless one way or another."
- "Bad decisions lead to disaster; the consequences of a mistake are catastrophic."
- "Even if it's depressing, I always prefer to think that things will go wrong, so I'll be prepared and less disappointed."

You may notice that the constructs illustrating this schema sometimes refer to an existential problem, sometimes to a solution, sometimes to a cost. This is quite normal; the Negativity/Pessimism schema is very versatile in terms of emotional coherence. This idea is very well illustrated in the *Coherence Therapy Practice Manual and Training Guide* by Ecker and Hulley (2019), found in the section on the functions of depression. The authors explain that depression is sometimes a consequence of an underlying schema and sometimes a solution in itself to avoid various types of suffering.

This Chapter's Main Points

- As we have mentioned several times throughout this book, the transformation (annulling and rewriting) of schemas through the therapeutic reconsolidation process (TRP) requires meeting precise criteria. To this end, in this chapter we have reorganized the 18 schemas identified by Young using the Schema Map (Figure 5.1) that we use in Coherence Therapy (CT). We have also used our Resources/Threats Matrix (Figure 1.1) to give examples of prediction specificities that can be found on the branches of the schema tree (our metaphor in Chapter 3). This precision is necessary to facilitate an error prediction experience.
- Of course, our aim is not to call into question the Schema Therapy (ST) model, which, as we have already mentioned, has proven to be extremely useful. Our intention is to revisit it from the perspective of the TRP.
- At the root of the Schema Map used in CT is the existential problem, that prediction of the worse suffering (for example, the unbearable suffering of abandonment). We define this existential problem as the prediction of vulnerability to specific sufferings. We consider five schemas to be linked to existential problems, since they predict worse suffering. In the ST model, they are also linked to failure to meet basic psychological needs. They are: Abandonment, Mistrust/Abuse, Emotional Deprivation, Social Isolation, Punishment.
- Worse apprehended suffering will automatically lead to the use of a solution to avoid the reactivation of this suffering (which is why the absence of a solution is often traumatic). We consider that nine schemas are linked to solutions. These are Unrelenting Standards, Subjugation, Self-Sacrifice, Approval-Seeking, Entitlement, Dependence, Enmeshment, Emotional Inhibition, Insufficient Self-Control/Self-Discipline. However, all these solutions come at a cost, which is why these schemas are described as dysfunctional strategies in ST (or at least, they have become so over time). In CT, they are

associated with less suffering which, although it may be significant, is evaluated as less unbearable than that which is avoided.

- In our transposition of schemas within the Schema Map of CT, four schemas are special cases. These are Defectiveness and Failure, on the one hand, and Vulnerability and Negativity/Pessimism, on the other.
    - Defectiveness and Failure schemas: Depending on our working viewpoint, these can be either predictions of major suffering or ways of putting into action a solution aimed at avoiding or limiting the experience of *even greater* suffering.
    - Vulnerability and Negativity/Pessimism schemas: These are often the consequence of operating with various schemas that deprive the individual of a sense of security, cut them off from their vitality, lead to various problems and conflicts, or even lead to exhaustion. They are also a reflection of the individual's highly skewed perception of people and situations, which is consistent with the context in which the perception was created.

Notes

1 In our first book (Côté & Cousineau, 2022), Chapter 6, Section 7 deals with the resistance encountered in the various stages of the TRP.
2 AEDP: Accelerated Experiential Dynamic Psychotherapy.
3 ISTDP: Intensive Short-Term Dynamic Psychotherapy.

Chapter 6
Transforming Schemas

To transform a schema, we need to engage the therapeutic reconsolidation process (TRP). And to do this, we first need to discover the schema's specific predictions, identify contradictory living knowledge or a means of creating contradictory information, then reactivate the target learning (the schema), creating a mismatch between the predictions of the schema and the facets of the person's experience that do not correspond to them, with the aim of producing a prediction error experience. We then simply need to repeat this juxtaposition, verbalizing it with the person two or three times, to permit the rewriting of the now destabilized schema (the schema's synapses are unlocked and able to be rewritten by a new emotional truth or schema).

It is important to point out that only a verification step confirming the presence of all three transformation markers will allow us to be sure that a schema has indeed been transformed. This step is designed to ensure 1) that the schema and its associated mode that were activated immediately on perception of a given trigger or context are no longer activated at all, 2) that the observable behavioral manifestations of this schema/mode no longer occur, and 3) that these two changes are maintained without any special effort, intervention or conditions being put in place to sustain them.

Let us see how this procedure plays out in concrete terms for the fundamental schemas listed in the previous chapter. That is, the schemas that involve predictions about the self, the world and others. Our Resources/Threats Matrix is an excellent tool for mapping these predictions into an organized perceptual system, enabling you to target the parts of the

DOI: 10.4324/9781003628125-8

schema that you can infirm with reality (contradictory living knowledge) and determine how to do so. Because only material that is perfectly contradictory (in content and emotional tone) to the specific predictions of the schema can create a prediction error experience for the person and destabilize their schema so that it can be annulled and rewritten. Precision is of the utmost importance here.

Several techniques exist in many therapeutic approaches to make the specific constructs of schemas explicit. The downward arrow technique is a good example, as long as it is guided by **feeling** and not executed in a purely intellectual form. As we often say in training and supervision, the clients know, but they don't know that they know. Any therapist-guided experience that puts the person in touch with their emotional truths and reveals them to the therapist will fulfill this objective. If, however, you would like to learn more about discovery techniques for precisely identifying these constructs, we invite you to consult books on Coherence Therapy ([CT]; Ecker et al., 2012, 2024; Ecker & Hulley, 2019; Côté & Cousineau, 2022).

Schemas Linked to Existential Problems

Abandonment schema. Here is an example of what the Abandonment schema of one of our clients expressed when she gave it full voice during discovery and integration work:

> I have to be continually vigilant about the possibility of rejection. It can happen at any time and with anyone: not being nice, funny, sparkly, brilliant or perfect is grounds for rejection. No wonder I live with so much anxiety. Every time someone is disappointed or, even worse, angry with me, I feel that terror or terrible apprehension I know so well from my life with Dad. My anger towards him is dangerous: if I go too far, he'll despise me, reject me, and it's the same with everyone else. It's so unbearable to go through this that I have to do everything I can to avoid it!
>
> Source: Authors' clinical work

This client's solution to avoid abandonment was to subjugate herself. We will come back to this later in the chapter.

Let's now analyze the structure of this Abandonment schema using our Resources/Threats Matrix:

External threat. *Behaviors of abandonment and rejection by loved ones.*
Internal threat. *Reactivation of episodic memories of subjective experiences of abandonment by the father; feeling anger is an internal threat because it can lead to reaching a point of no return in confrontation, triggering contempt and rejection from others.*
External resources. *Prediction of loss of resources in the event of abandonment.*
Internal resources. *Prediction of inability to tolerate an experience of abandonment or reactivation of trauma.*

In a case like this, the transformation work will have to take place at several levels in the schema, so that the symptoms of Subjugation (functional symptom: implementation of the solution) and anxiety (symptom without function) dissipate:

External threat. *This prediction is based on the father's behaviors, and generalized to everyone else. A shift could be created quite easily by getting the person to declare the predictions of their schema (the above quotation) out loud, experientially (in imagination) to a loved one who did not engage in abandonment or rejection behavior in a situation where the client was imperfect in some way. The aim of this experiment would not be to create a prediction error experience about the possibility of rejection, but about the certainty that everyone will react exactly like her father in the face of her imperfections. Entering into a prediction error and rewriting this over-generalization with a heartfelt contradictory experience of this kind is likely to cause the person to be confronted with the harsh reality that, if everyone does not behave this way, then it means their attachment figure was incapable of loving them unconditionally (for example). This very direct contact with loss that requires the patient to mourn for the parent they wish they had can not only provoke resistance, but also requires that the client be accompanied through the grieving process so that it can be named, legitimized, accepted and completed.*
Internal threat. *The work here will take place in two phases. As long as the patient's episodic emotional memory retains overwhelming traumatic material, she will feel terror and will have to resort to solutions to avoid this emotion. The aim is to check with the person whether it is possible to revisit, in imagination, one or more significant episodes of abandonment from her father, in this case. This is done at the client's own pace, and often progressively. As she comes into contact with the therapist's kind and compassionate presence, she begins to be able to tolerate contact with the traumatic material. Once avoidance is overcome, a structured reenactment experience aimed at establishing a sense of power can be guided. It can be the exercise "I am in memory," for example (Ecker et al., 2012, 2024; Côté & Cousineau, 2022), or other relevant experiences in which, through imagery, the patient can change the story. Once the emotional episodic memory has been defused, it will be simply a bad memory when it is reactivated by a stimulus. The internal threat of post-traumatic emotional flooding is thus eliminated.*

Then, for working on the prediction that anger leads to going too far and provoking rejection or abandonment, the process is quite similar to that described for the ***External threat****. The therapist could guide an experiment in which the patient declares, in imagery, her prediction to a loved one who clearly does not behave like the father. For example, "I am convinced that you are exactly like my father: if I let my anger go too far, you will reject and despise me exactly as he did." This creates a mismatch that allows an experience of predictive error to occur (the patient will experience contradictory knowledge to the effect that this person would never behave this way). There may also be another avenue if the original attachment figure (the father in this case), has never actually abandoned the client permanently, even though he has caused the client to experience very intense rejection or contempt. The mismatch detection experience would then lie at the level of the certainty that confrontation always results in permanent abandonment, since the parent has never actually carried out this threat.*

External resources. *Here, contradictory knowledge highlighting that should the dreaded abandonment occur, the person would still have a good support network, seems to us an avenue to be explored to create a mismatch. The vivid feeling that a safety net exists, if this is indeed the case for the person, can be a powerful experience to help tolerate the possibility of abandonment (since no one is immune to this experience).*

Internal resources. *In the same vein, the person may have had various poignant and revealing experiences in which they were able to draw on internal resources (such as self-compassion, resilience) to cope with rejection or abandonment. If these experiences are not readily available to create a mismatch, then it is entirely appropriate to use incremental learning by teaching techniques such as self-compassion, then explicitly creating experiences that draw the person's attention to their prediction of being completely helpless to cope with this suffering and at the same time to their experience of being able to draw on new, effective resources that make the suffering bearable. The temporary nature of this type of suffering (it does not last indefinitely) can also serve as contradictory knowledge; the mismatch would then be created based on the prediction that suffering caused by abandonment never stops (this prediction may be implicit but could be made explicit if the person feels it to be true), whereas in the person's own real life experience, they have learned that this type of suffering does eventually come to an end.*

Mistrust/Abuse Schema. Here is an example of what the Mistrust/Abuse schema of one of our clients expressed when she gave it full voice during discovery and integration work:

> Every time I say what's on my mind, every time I show off my skills, and worse, every time someone compliments me, you can't tolerate it, you attack me and humiliate me. It destroys

me completely and I'm convinced I'm less than nothing. That look in your eyes takes away my will to live. I have no way of escaping your wickedness; no matter what I do or say, you're stronger than I am, and you'll always win, have the last word. There's no force in the universe that can stop you unless you decide to.

Source Authors' clinical experience

Let's now analyze the structure of this Mistrust/Abuse schema using our Resources/Threats Matrix:

External threat. *The schema predicts that her mother's aggression and humiliation of her are triggered by the expression of her thoughts, the display of her skills, or simply their recognition by others. The schema also predicts that this threat is all-powerful.*

Internal threat. *The schema anticipates a feeling of being completely destroyed, of having no value to the point of losing the will to live, which is terrifying. The schema also predicts that the simple desire to exist and have value is dangerous, because of what it triggers* (external threat).

External resources. *The schema predicts that no external resource is powerful enough to protect the person from the all-powerful* external threat.

Internal resources. *The schema predicts that the person has no internal resources to protect her from aggression and humiliation.*

This schema structure is interesting, because the predictions at various points in the Resources/Threats Matrix flow from one another. They are the main beams of the building; by moving them, we transform the whole building.

External threat. *When you hear about the mother's behavior towards the client, how do you perceive the mother?* Do you *see her as an all-powerful force? If you look at it through your Schema Therapy (ST) lens, you will probably conclude that this person is attacking and humiliating your patient in Overcompensator mode because her own vulnerabilities have been triggered. Imagine what would happen if you could get your client to see her in this light, too.*

In this client's case, the mismatch detection experience occurred when the therapist led her to realize that her mother's aggressive behaviors all happened in situations where she was not the center of attention. The decisive detail, which could act as contradictory knowledge to the schema's prediction, was that a person must feel extremely fragile, small and vulnerable to have to resort to such spectacular and cruel solutions in order to feel worthwhile and secure. Without being led by the therapist to get to the bottom of things, the client might never have questioned her mother's motives for counter-attacking in this way. A downward arrow exercise, always well connected to the feeling, can also serve to make this contradictory knowledge explicit and put it at odds with the client's schema's perception of her mother as an all-powerful being.

Everything that rests on the client's construct of maternal omnipotence may crumble with this paradigm shift, but even after this transformation is complete, other beams still need to be moved.

Internal threat. *To bring the patient to have an experience in which the prediction of being destroyed and losing the will to live, is out of step with reality, it is necessary either to find in her memory a clear and unequivocal experience in which she did not feel this way after a verbal aggression, or to first build her internal resources to create the experience from scratch. It would also be interesting, for the prediction portion about her sense of worth, to have her feel both the worth she has in the eyes of other attachment figures, along with an experience of psychological aggression relived in imagination.*

It is often useful to draw clients' attention to the fact that different significant attachment figures used in the imagery exercise are looking at the same person (being abused and called names). Some figures legitimize their needs and worthiness, while others denigrate them from a radically different perspective (incongruence); they cannot all be correct simultaneously.

The imagery rescripting exercise described in Chapter 4 (van der Wijngaart, 2021) can also be used for this purpose. As we have mentioned several times in this book, bringing into question the client's value as a person as defined by the cruel or denigrating gaze of a parent often leads the individual to come into contact with painful realizations about the parent, such as the parent's inability to love the client and the necessity for the client to grieve for the parent they needed but didn't have. Many clients will then avoid feeling the healthy despair of grief, which is necessary for their progress, and will need to be accompanied in this process with much gentleness and compassion.

If traumatic implicit emotional episodic memories are part of the perceived threats, they must be transformed so that they are no longer part of the internal landscape, using the same techniques as described at the beginning of this chapter in the section on the Abandonment schema.

External resources. *Even in cases where the people close to the client do not actually defend them in situations of aggression, it is rare for a client to be totally isolated. It is possible to have the client revisit a scene of aggression using imagery, placing all the external resources that are significant to them in the scene, be they loved ones, authority figures, law-enforcement figures, or even religious figures if they are subjectively perceived as having power. Of course, the therapist can also be included, as he or she represents an external resource for the person when the therapeutic alliance is solid and strongly felt by the patient. Once the scene of aggression has been revisited, the person can then ask each significant figure for their opinion on what has just happened and take the time to speak and integrate the responses and their subjective meaning.*

Internal resources. *As mentioned in the section on internal threat, these resources may be represented explicitly in imagery, or they may be built up first in therapy and then used in an imagery exercise. It is quite possible that, under the therapist's kind and compassionate gaze, the person will be able to get in touch with their internal resources, something they won't always be able to do if they are only led to revisit memories of aggression in imagery, as they will be rather overwhelmed by feelings of helplessness and panic in these situations. It is often useful to draw the individual's attention to their internal resources when they describe supporting a loved one or child, or asserting themself in situations where there was no aggression, and then to represent these internal resources clearly in imagery exercises involving scenes with aggression, in order to create a mismatch (with the schema that predicts that these internal resources do not exist). Indeed, this is exactly what van der Wijngaart (2021) does in imagery when he asks the patient to revisit a job interview experience.*

Emotional Deprivation Schema. Here is an example of what the Emotional Deprivation schema of one of our clients expressed when he gave it full voice during discovery and integration work:

> Nothing's changed: it's still my role to be the strong one, I'm not allowed to be unwell or cause problems. You're all just like Mom; if I let it show that I'm anxious (that I'm not doing well), I'll end up all alone again without help or support, just like when I was little, because I'll become a burden for you. I have to avoid this at all costs! I must continue to hide my suffering and help; insomnia is still my worst enemy because I can't hide it.
>
> Source: Authors' clinical work

Let us now analyze the structure of this Emotional Deprivation schema using our Resources/Threats Matrix:

External threat. *The Emotional Deprivation schema does not usually include a clear external threat as do Mistrust/Abuse and Abandonment schemas, where there is usually a clearly defined behavior that is threatening. This will make perfect sense when we analyze the internal threat component. Nevertheless, the lack of response from attachment figures, or from other external human resources, could be considered a form of external threat.*

Internal threat. *In this case, the schema predicts that it is when the patient is unwell, feels tired or weak, or is the cause of a problem, that he will experience contact with emotional deprivation. Another internal threat associated with this schema is the subjective experience of emptiness, or black hole, that so many emotionally deprived people describe feeling when their needs are ignored.*

External resources. *The schema here makes a generalization based on this man's experiences in his attachment relationship with his mother. The prediction anticipates that external resources will always be as poor as they were when he was young, whether the situation involves the original attachment figure (here the mother) or not.*

Internal resources. *This schema predicts that, without the support of loved ones, he will find himself as helpless as a young child, and so this construct defines a reality in which he possesses the same internal resources as he did when he was young, as if they had not developed.*

Note that many Emotional Deprivation schemas will tend to include constructs predicting that no matter how much they have developed internal resources (skills, kindness, engagement with others, etc.) they are still insufficient for others to love and support them or pay attention to them, which keeps them constantly unsatisfied.

Let us now look at how mismatches can be created to lead the person to experience a prediction error in the different facets of a schema like this one:

External threat. *In this client's case, it was indeed the realization that emotional deprivation was not manifested at all in his current attachment relationships (his spouse and friends) that created a mismatch for this schema and enabled the mismatch detection and rewriting experiences to take place.*

Internal threat. *Here again, a disconfirming experience in which being perceived as suffering, tired or weak does not result in the absence of a kind response from those around you, can create the desired mismatch. The paradigm shift we are looking for here is that fatigue or suffering are no longer threats because they no longer trigger behaviors of indifference from others.*

On the other hand, given that failures of emotional connection and ruptures of shared reality are an integral part of all relational experiences, it is inevitable that the person will be confronted with them. The mismatch sought in these situations will be in the subjective experience in the present, as an adult, compared to what was subjectively felt as a child. It is only when a person is able to fully feel these unpleasant experiences as an adult that this gap with the prediction, "Nothing has changed, every time my needs are ignored I feel exactly the same hole, the same emptiness I felt as a child" can be transformed. This mismatch can, for example, be achieved with a two-screen technique, in which the person is led to observe a scene where they were in contact with their Emotional Deprivation as a child and a recent scene experienced in their adult life and to observe in precisely what ways the two subjective experiences are different.

External resources. *Experiences in which the person can be made fully aware that certain people are able, most of the time, to consider their needs, show sincere interest in them, repair ruptures in shared reality or emotional connection, will be experiences* *that contradict the part of the schema that predicts that these people do not exist, or exist only to a limited extent. It is also interesting to get the person to observe that external resources have become available in their life, and that they have a "safety net" into which they can fall if a momentary void is created in their relational contact with an attachment figure, which may not have been the case when they were a child.*

Internal resources. *Once again, an experiment can be guided in which a mismatch is made between the person's perception of being as deprived as a child, and the realization that their adult reality is quite different. As for the prediction that no matter how hard the person tries or how much they are able to do, it is never sufficient to avoid or fill the emotional deprivation, contradictory experiences can be sought out to make it clear to the individual that it is by making better relational choices that they will find answers to their needs, and thus avoid constantly remaining unsatisfied.*

Social Isolation Schema. Here is an example of what one of our clients' Social Isolation schema expressed when she gave it full voice during discovery and integration work:

> I never fit in at school, and I still don't fit in at work. Everybody still sees me as an alien, and when you see it too you're going to ridicule and reject me. No matter how hard I try to fit in, it doesn't make any difference, I always end up all alone in my corner because I'm not interesting enough. Nobody really understands me. It's horrible to feel all alone in the world all the time and to see that everyone else finds their place somewhere where they're comfortable and accepted.
>
> Source: Authors' clinical work

Let us now analyze the structure of this Social Isolation schema using our Resources/Threats Matrix:

External threat. *In this type of schema, the main threat is being seen by others, which brings rejection or ostracism. In many cases, as in this example, past experiences of intimidation also lead to the anticipation that the situation will escalate to insults or public humiliation.*

Internal threat. *The experience of being isolated and apart from the group. Knowing how crucial access to the group has been to our survival for millennia, it is easy to understand why the feeling of being cut off from groups is anxiety-provoking and distressing in a deeply primitive way.*

External resources. *The schema perceives access to external resources as very limited.*

Internal resources. *As is often the case, this schema includes self-attribution constructs to give coherence to social exclusion. Here, the schema predicts that it is by not being interesting enough that the person is causing their exclusion from the group.*

Let us now look at how mismatches can be created to guide the person into experiencing a prediction error in the different facets of a schema like this one:

External threat. *One way of removing power or legitimacy from the external threat would be, as with the Mistrust/Abuse schema shown at the beginning of this chapter, to elucidate the real motivations of people who have shown bullying or rejection behaviors, always in an experiential mode, of course. It is also possible to create a mismatch between the extent of rejection or bullying behaviors in a schoolyard, for example, and those adopted by work colleagues, provided, of course, that they are clearly contrasting. While this may not completely eliminate the external threat, it could at least bring about a transformation in the schema, in which the magnitude of the threat diminishes in relation to the way it was perceived in the context of school.*

Internal threat. *As we have mentioned several times, if implicit emotional episodic memories are traumatic in nature, we will need to work experientially to defuse them, so that their activation by social triggers no longer leads to emotional flooding and the threat is thus eliminated. Once again, experiencing rejection or exclusion as an adult and bringing this experience into an experiential mismatch with the child's feelings, can create enough of a mismatch to transform the perception of exclusion into an experience that is still painful, but one that is less devastating than it once was.*

External resources. *The therapist is an excellent source of contradictory material. By taking care to build a therapeutic relationship in which the patient feels a very real belonging to a subgroup, every experience in which the person feels genuinely understood in her reality by the therapist, and co-existing in a common relational space, can serve as a contradictory experience to juxtapose with the prediction of the "nobody understands me" schema, for example.*

Internal resources. *Very often, people with this type of schema bring situations of exclusion on themselves, by lacking the social skills to promote their inclusion. Teaching social skills is tantamount to increasing internal resources, which in turn increase the individual's chances of having a contradictory experience of inclusion, giving them an opportunity to mismatch the schema's prediction of systematic rejection.*

Punishment Schema. Here is an example of what the Punishment schema of one of our clients expressed when he gave it full voice during discovery and integration work:

> You're just like my father: if I don't live up to your expectations, you'll get angry, think I'm no good, judge me and even attack me, and I'll end up all alone with my pain, my terror and being overwhelmed by these emotions! I'm still so small and vulnerable

in front of your anger. I have to avoid this at all costs by doing everything I can to meet your expectations.

Let us now analyze the structure of this Punishment schema using our Resources/Threats Matrix:

External threat. *This schema predicts that disappointing others provokes their anger and is punished by verbal or physical violence and some form of belittling or humiliation and rejection.*

Internal threat. *These threats are the subjective experience of feeling the pain and overwhelming terror of undergoing such treatment from another person.*

External resources. *This schema predicts that the individual will find himself alone as a result of the punishment, which also suggests that he will be alone to face it.*

Internal resources. *The schema perceives current internal resources as being the same as those of a vulnerable toddler, suggesting that this self-perception has not been updated since childhood.*

Let us now look at how mismatches can be created to lead the person to experience a prediction error in the different facets of a schema like this one:

External threat. *The schema operates according to a generalization which predicts that everyone will behave like the father did. It is at the level of this generalization that the mismatch can be created by juxtaposing the emotional truth of the schema with an experience in which someone clearly did not behave like the father in a situation where the client did not meet expectations and would expect to be punished accordingly. It is, of course, possible to create a mismatch if the father himself has changed and no longer reacts by punishing his son when he disappoints him. The mismatch can be created using a juxtaposing imagery technique with two screens. On the first screen, the patient imagines a memory of being punished as a child by their father after having disappointed him, which elicits a feeling of terror. On the second screen, he imagines a memory as an adult of disappointing someone else (or the father if he has changed) without being punished after having stated out loud the prediction of his schema.*

Internal threat. *As we have mentioned several times, if implicit emotional episodic memories are traumatic in nature, we will need to work experientially to defuse them, so that their activation by situations of disappointment or angry or judgmental reactions in others no longer brings on emotional flooding and the threat is thus eliminated. Once again, feeling the anger of others as an adult and bringing the experience into an experiential mismatch with a child's feelings can create enough of a shift to transform the perception of punishment into an experience that is still painful but less devastating than it once was.*

External resources. *It is possible that the existence of solid, healthy relationships could make the experience very different for the person should they find themself attacked* *again. It is even possible that this actually occurred and can thus serve as contradictory knowledge in an imagery juxtaposition. van der Wijngaart's (2021) exercise can also serve to perform this task admirably, providing a highly committed and proactive external resource to take up the defense of the patient, prevent the punishment from taking place and even denounce the injustice of the mistreatment inflicted.*

Internal resources. *There is an imagery exercise that we like to use to uncover the internal resources that the schema predicts to be absent. We ask the patient to imagine that their child, or a child very dear to them, receives the punishment. As an adult with internal resources that were not available in childhood or adolescence, the client will feel compelled to mobilize these resources spontaneously in this exercise. Then, all we need to do is draw the person's attention to their current experience of having these internal resources, which is at odds with the prediction of the schema (according to which they are insufficient or absent).*

Schemas Linked to Solutions (Examples)

We have just explored transforming schemas that are linked to existential problems. What about applying the TRP to schemas linked to solutions?

These schemas are actually adaptive solutions requiring the production of certain symptoms. Therefore, the clinical task when applying the TRP is generally to guide the discovery and integration of these constructs in order to render explicit the underlying existential problem that makes the solution necessary to the person's functioning by allowing the person to avoid suffering that is even worse than that of grappling with the symptoms on a daily basis (see Appendix 1 for more on schema coherence). Consider these two examples of interventions that address schemas linked to solutions: Unrelenting Standards and Subjugation schemas.

Unrelenting Standards Schema. Let us use the example of clients who firmly stick to a position where they minimize the costs generated by a coping solution such as the Unrelenting Standards schema. These clients often invest the solution in a deeply egosyntonic way, as if there were no other way of functioning. Intervention is possible from exactly this angle. Let us look at an example from a client who has this schema and who comes to therapy not because she wants to let go of her rules, but rather because she is burned out:

> I'm convinced that there's only one way to do things, and that's to do them perfectly. Even knowing all the anxiety it causes me, it's the only way to keep the love and esteem of my loved ones, just like with my parents.
>
> Source: Authors' clinical work

This is the type of person who often consults us to find ways of getting back on their feet and continuing to live according to their preferred strategy. The transformation work requires a great deal of finesse, so as not to tip over into confrontation (either gentle or forceful), and thus into a form of cognitive restructuring. The aim here is to gradually bring the person to integrate their schema's pro-symptom position, and then to lead them towards the contradictory knowledge they already possess, because we know that this solution is not really the only one available to them, and that it probably does not produce all the results hoped for. The two sources of incongruent material are therefore, on the one hand, knowledge that contradicts the belief that there are no other solutions for this problem and, on the other, knowledge about the results this solution actually achieves.

The therapist can then encourage the patient, for example, to make an overt statement to her loved ones, assuming her schema coherent position:

> I'm convinced that there's only one way to do things, and that's to do them perfectly. Even knowing all the anxiety it causes me, it's the only way to keep your love and esteem, just like with you, Mom and Dad.
>
> Source: Authors' clinical work

The therapist can then gently bring her to feel, one loved one at a time, whether she has indeed succeeded in obtaining the love she is longing for through this strategy. The patient may then come into contact with a confronting emotional truth, a form of Emotional Deprivation, for example, and work can continue in this new direction. In these cases, it is possible that the existential problem is insoluble (for example, an attachment figure is simply not available for the relationship you are hoping for and will not change). Once this has been brought to consciousness and integrated, it is then possible to continue the transformation by accompanying the patient through a grieving process.

The client may also be led to question her loved ones, using imagery, to ascertain with them whether this solution is the only way to make herself loved and valuable in their eyes. It is quite possible that this experience will lead her to realize that while this may be true for some loved ones, it is absolutely not the case for others; the overgeneralization aspect of the schema will then become explicit.

In a case like this, it is also often enough to get the person to make an overt statement of their solution, emphasizing this egosyntonic position in relation to the costs (stress, exhaustion, isolation, sacrifice, etc.), and to question them so that they feel whether all the parts of the self are really in agreement with what they have just asserted. In this way, another form of contradictory knowledge is created, that is, those parts of the self which no longer agree with such high costs to avoid suffering, and which want to see a change. We can then continue by working on the existential problem, which will correspond to one or more of the schemas listed in that category.

It is also possible that the solution schema reflects a construction of reality that took place at a very early age, when psychoaffective development and internal resources had only a very limited range of possibilities or solutions. As one of us (PC) likes to say, the child adapts with the means at hand! When the person has not experienced any updating of the constructs concerning available solutions, the perception remains exactly the same in adulthood. This can be done simply with experiential psychoeducation or a simple reflection. One of the classic examples in the *Coherence Therapy Practice Manual* (Ecker & Hulley, 2019) is that of a client who discovered that she completely erased herself and lived an extremely monotonous and boring life to prevent her narcissistic and invasive mother from taking everything away from her because, according to her schema, there were no walls, no protection, between her and her mother. The therapist, once this schema had been made quite explicit and integrated by his client, simply commented: "Have you thought about not telling Mom?" The client, stunned, was in shock; the part of the self that inhabited this perspective had never realized that this possibility existed (that she could, by her silence, erect a wall between her mother and herself, and that her mother could not appropriate what she did not know about). A new solution had just appeared, and it changed the situation completely. The whole part of the schema that was based on the perception that there was only one possible solution (fading away), suddenly collapsed. So, keep an eye out, while you are still keeping one foot in your own reality (versus that of your patients), to see if a solution of this type could completely change the situation as perceived through a schema, bearing in mind that what may seem obvious to a Healthy Adult, may be totally foreign to the reality of a Vulnerable Child. Especially if these two realities (that of the possibilities perceived by a Healthy Adult and that of the possibilities perceived by a Vulnerable Child) have never met in the same field of conscious attention or the same well embodied and felt experience.

Subjugation Schema. Let us continue the exercise with an example of the Subjugation schema:

> I'm absolutely convinced that anger automatically means that everything will fall apart. I absolutely have to be pleasant and kind; it's the only way I won't lose everything.
>
> Source: Authors' clinical work

The therapist guided this patient to experience two types of contradictory knowledge leading to the transformation of this schema. On the one hand, the knowledge that even if his children had experienced the worst of his irritability or imperfection, his relationship with them was still good and he was loved by them, sincerely. On the other hand, despite decades of a relationship marked by his father's angry outbursts and the countless ways in which he had provoked it, in addition to the hatred he had felt towards his father at times, this relationship had never actually collapsed. The client's paradigm shifted when he came into contact with this prediction error—he realized that relationships were not made up of just avoidance of anger, and that his father's tantrums did not mean there was an absence of love. He realized that the relationship with his father, as with his children, was not limited to the presence or absence of anger, and that it was made up of many facets that remained real and tangible even when anger was part of it.

This illustrates the point we made in Chapter 5. In most cases, the transformation of a solution-related schema requires targeting the underlying existential problem that makes this solution necessary (perception of threats/resources). It is therefore not necessary to illustrate the TRP with all the solution schemas in ST, as the TRP framework remains exactly the same with all of them: discovering and integrating the existential problem that makes the solution and symptoms necessary, then guiding the unlearning through well-targeted juxtaposition experiments, all with the utmost respect for the person's window of tolerance.

Special Cases

Defectiveness Schema. According to our clinical experience, any serious issue concerning one or more of the schemas related to existential problems will almost systematically be accompanied by the Defectiveness schema. We invite you to conceptualize it as the tip of an iceberg. This schema is most often perceived as a self-image shaped by traumatic or harmful experiences. How does an individual come to maintain such a self-image, and to hold on to it no matter how many important validating experiences they subsequently have in healthy relationships? Why does this self-definition tend to come up again and again in therapy, when the therapist is explicitly looking at the person in a kind, worth-validating way?

The answer is simple: Because in all these cases, it is necessary to maintain this negative self-image to avoid suffering that is even greater than that of living with the feeling of worthlessness. That is why we say that the Defectiveness schema represents a form of solution. It is the tip of the iceberg; all the rest of what is immersed in the depths of implicit memory remains to be discovered, integrated and transformed. Until this is done, self-attributions and low-value self-perceptions will persist:

> Everyone who loves me is like Mom and Ex, so that means you too Partner. If I let myself believe I'm worthy, you'll throw a tantrum, laugh at me some more, humiliate me, attack me. The only

> way to avoid this is to agree with you and believe I'm worthless, no good, not interesting, insignificant and to put myself down to protect myself from your attacks.
>
> Source: Authors' clinical work

This is what was lurking beneath the tip of the iceberg for this person, and which generated an ongoing self-deprecating discourse in his current love relationship, through generalization. The existential problem in this case predicts that existing by giving oneself value provokes anger, attack and humiliation, which this patient experienced abundantly in his attachment relationship with his mother and, later, with his abusive ex-spouse. We see here a classic illustration of the type of situation in which countless children find themselves when in the care of a toxic parent. In order to shift the locus of control to reduce the feeling of helplessness and vulnerability in the face of violence or abuse, the child fragments reality by making an attribution to self, which then becomes an automatic conviction. The work of discovery and integration enables the person to make explicit once again that this is not a simple identity construction: it is the means they found to adapt to a toxic environment. By siding with the aggressor, they reduce aggression and avoid finding themself vulnerable and alone.

For this client, the transformation of this schema required bringing together several contradictory cognitions and experiences in a single space of experience and attention, as is often the case with attachment traumas, complex or otherwise. On the one hand, the client realized that his current love dynamics were not at all the same as they were with his mother and ex-wife, which helped counteract the overgeneralization. On the other hand—and this aspect is not reflected in the above example of emotional truth—the client also realized that healthy detachment from what does not belong to him in other people's problems (in this case his romantic partner's problems) no longer results in him being retraumatized by experiencing the overwhelming feelings associated with Emotional Deprivation. He therefore realized that he had the necessary internal and external resources to be self-sufficient, as he was taking this distance until he could once again get closer to his partner. These two transformations thus enabled him to settle into a Healthy Adult mode in his current love relationship since he no longer needed to resort to the self-denigration of the Defectiveness schema to function in his relationships.

If this perspective on self-image issues (Defectiveness schema[1]) has created a mismatch for you, we invite you to explore, in your clinical interventions, the coherence and function of these issues as adaptive features rather than seeing self-image as a static entity to be addressed directly. It is always surprising to see how many patients resist changing their negative self-image, despite an abundance of feedback to the contrary—one criticism outweighs a thousand compliments! In cases where our schemas have not led us to almost perfectly duplicate a toxic initial environment through identical relational choices, why do we so adamantly cling to a negative perception of ourselves? It is a question worth pondering.

Vulnerability Schema. As mentioned in the previous chapter, the Vulnerability schema is very often linked to the cost of a solution put into place to avoid worse suffering. In our Schema Map (Figure 5.1), it would therefore usually be found in the symptom without function section. As it is most often a consequence of a schema linked to a solution whose function is to avoid the reactivation of another, more fundamental schema, the path to transformation of the Vulnerability schema is less direct. It will therefore not be possible to modify the Vulnerability schema without taking into account what makes it necessary to maintain it.

Let us take a look at a concrete clinical situation. The client, a man in his thirties, had already been successfully treated for panic disorder by a cognitive-behavioral therapist a few years previously. The patient had subsequently consulted a schema therapist for issues relating to an excessive need for control. This therapy had been completed two years earlier, when the patient called on her (the schema therapist) again because his panic disorder had reappeared, and he was no longer able to control it with what he had learned in his first therapy.

The therapist, who has since learned about the TRP, now works on the assumption that the symptom is coherent: How is this anxiety-panic coherent? Her first step is to explore with the client, using mental imagery, the context preceding the recent reappearance of the symptom. The client describes the following situation. He lives in a different town from his parents, and during a telephone call with his mother, she insists that he come and visit her, despite the fact that he has just spoken about his hectic schedule. His Subjugation schema has always made him apprehensive about disappointing his mother and provoking her anger and even rejection (very painful, even if temporary). At first, the client makes no connection between this telephone conversation and his anxious reaction. But the therapist is alerted by a subsequent comment the client reported making to his partner after the call: he expresses his dissatisfaction that his mother doesn't take others into account, that she only thinks of herself, and so on. He is surprised to realize this when the therapist reflects it back to him. The discovery work that follows will reveal the full coherence of the panic symptom. Experiencing anger is an internal threat, since it would lead to confronting Mom, which would lead to disappointment, anger, and rejection on her part, something he predicts will be emotionally intolerable. The solution, then, is not to become aware of his anger, and not to confront Mom on the basis of it. But the attempt to suppress this anger is more or less effective: it is felt (comment to his partner), but cannot be expressed in a clear, direct and assertive way to Mom. As regularly emphasized in ISTDP,[2] this conflict, played out at an unconscious (implicit) level, and manifests itself as anxiety, which in this context becomes a symptom without a function. In this particular case, the functional symptom, the one that puts into action the solution of not being directly aware of his anger towards Mom, is to interpret his reaction as a panic disorder.

This example illustrates how transforming the Vulnerability schema requires patient and insightful discovery work. But once the coherence of the symptom has been identified and integrated, the transformation will, as always, require the execution of the TRP. For example, the client must experience a prediction error concerning the level of threat posed by the experience of confronting Mom and the resources he now possesses to be able to do so.

Conclusion

We have just examined, in the last three chapters, what schema transformation requires. It is not linked to any specific therapeutic technique, but rather to a framework that guides the TRP.

As we have pointed out earlier in this book, Young's schemas are very much in line with the characteristics that define a predictive memory. Memory transformation requires that, once reactivated, the now explicit predictive memory come into contact with elements that trigger the experience of a deeply felt prediction error. It is to this dimension of experience that you must pay attention when using the therapeutic technique of your choice.

In this sense, we hope that using our Resources/Threats Matrix (Figure 1.1) as we suggest can help you to specify the target predictions to aim for in the transformation work, as well as the type of experiences that could serve to create a mismatch and the essential experience of a prediction error.

ST and CT are based on very different paradigms. However, certain parallels can be drawn. In ST, the challenge of meeting fundamental psychological needs is at the heart of the model, and failure to meet these needs is the source of suffering, which is avoided by using dysfunctional strategies. Dysfunctional strategies never provide a truly satisfactory response to these needs and are costly.

In the case of CT, Ecker has always been opposed to working from a predefined list of schemas, as we do in ST. For him, every prediction is a schema, which means there is an infinite number of possibilities. And since therapeutic reconsolidation requires each mismatch to correspond perfectly to each problematic model of reality, he prefers not to provide predetermined categories, encouraging therapists to figure out these details for themselves, learning them directly from their clients. When a schema predicts worse suffering, a solution is used to avoid it (if one exists). The solution entails costs that are qualified as lesser suffering. But it is always the discovery work that will serve to specify the nature of the existential problem and of the solutions, or the lack thereof.

Ecker and his team make just one exception to this rejection of predetermined categories: what is called the Defectiveness schema in ST, which they identify by its main symptom, a tenacious low sense of self-worth. This is because the constructs of this type of schema, as we have mentioned many times in this book, tend to be not only complex, but protected by aggressive and cunning experiential avoidance strategies. They have developed a non-exhaustive list of fourteen possible emotional truths that underpin this type of schema and make self-deprecation necessary to maintain (Ecker & Hulley, 2019).

Despite these differences between the two approaches, it remains possible, as we have seen in the last two chapters, to apply the Schema Map (Figure 5.1) to Young's schemas with its prediction of worse suffering, a solution (or lack thereof) to a situation, leading to certain responses (functional symptoms) and their consequences (functionless symptoms). This can greatly facilitate developing an understanding that could lead to a more controlled use of the TRP.

One of the most important points to remember from this chapter as you discover the world of possibilities open to you for schema transformation—in addition, of course to the basic notions listed in the previous paragraph—is that early maladaptive schemas are very broad categories. They are a bit like filing cabinet drawers; when you open them, you might find just one or two folders, easy enough to pin down. In other cases, the experiences that make up your patient's life course will have built up numerous folders with complex content, one tangled up in the other. In the end, the framework remains the same: discover, integrate and transform these paradigm files with the process of memory reconsolidation. It will simply require greater attention to the specificity of the files identified in the filing cabinet drawers. In this, we walk wholeheartedly alongside you, with our own clients, with the common goal of alleviating suffering and, in so doing, making human relationships more harmonious and healthy.

This Chapter's Main Points

- This chapter focuses on the schema transformation step. To do this, we review the therapeutic reconsolidation process (TRP): discover the specific prediction of the schema to be transformed, identify contradictory living knowledge, then reactivate the target learning (the schema) so that it is experienced concurrently with the information that mismatches the prediction, and the mismatch can be registered subjectively as a prediction error experience. This juxtaposition can then be repeated to facilitate the rewriting of the now-destabilized schema (the schema's synapses are unlocked and able to be rewritten by a new emotional truth or schema).
- In this chapter, we present clinical examples of schema interventions based on TRP principles. Respecting our Schema Map (Figure 5.1), the intervention takes into account the categories of schemas we defined in Chapter 5: schemas related to existential problems, schemas related to solutions and to special cases.
- When we work on the schemas linked to existential problems, we are at the heart of the predictive model of the worse suffering. These

schemas form the basis of the Schema Map leading to solutions and their consequences. For each of these five schemas, we give examples of predictions based on the Resources/Threats Matrix (Figure 1.1), followed by examples of possible mismatches that could lead to a prediction error experience. If these schemas are transformed, the solutions will no longer be necessary—the whole building will collapse.

- As for solution schemas, their function is adaptive, a way of avoiding the worse suffering associated with existential issues. These solutions require the production of certain symptoms. The suggested intervention is, first of all, discovery work to clarify the function of the symptom and to integrate the subjective reason why it is necessary to produce it. We can then seek knowledge that challenges this justification (updating predictions about resources and threats), enabling the schema to be transformed. Examples of work with the Unrelenting Standards and Subjugation schemas are presented.
- We give examples of interventions on the Defectiveness and Vulnerability schemas which, as explained in Chapter 5, are special cases according to our way of presenting schemas.
- Finally, we conclude this chapter by suggesting some parallels that can be drawn between the Schema Therapy and Coherence Therapy models.

Notes

1 This would also be true for issues related to self-confidence (Failure schema).
2 Intensive Short-Term Dynamic Psychotherapy.

Appendix I

The following is a translation of the Schema Map description given in Côté and Cousineau (2022, pp. 100–107).

The Schema Map

The perspective we are presenting is a constructivist framework: the elements that make up any model of reality, whether the model is problematic or not, are constructs. We also use the terms "emotional truths," and "subjective embodied truths." These terms simply mean that, whatever their nature, constructs are subjectively experienced as true. The co-creators of Coherence Therapy have organized constructs into six orders (Ecker & Hulley, 1996), and the first four orders have been retained to form a framework for case studies and research (Ecker et al., 2012, 2024). These orders correspond to the four levels used in the Schema Map (Appendix.1). In day-to-day clinical practice, it is not necessary to refer to orders of constructs by number: all you need to do is clarify the existential problem and its associated suffering, the presence or absence of a solution to the existential problem, the means put in place to execute the solution (the resulting symptoms), and the situations that this problematic model of reality deems relevant. That is enough information to grasp the coherence of a model of reality.

As you can see in Appendix 1, the tree metaphor is very useful for finding your way around this framework. Let us start with the base of the schematic tree: the roots.

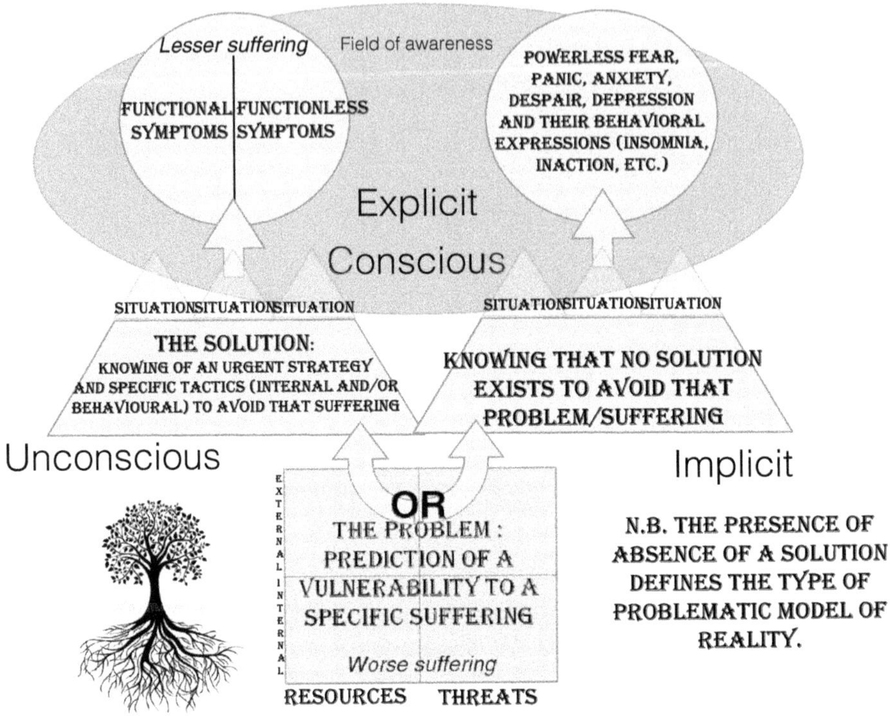

Figure A1 Schema Map

The Existential Problem

From the very beginning of our lives, we start constructing our perceptions by learning, either statistically or from traumatic experiences, how our internal and external environments work. At the root of this learning is the existential problem, which is defined as a learned construct that informs the individual that the world, the self or others operate according to specific rules and cause significant suffering for the individual. For example, during a separation from a parent, a child who experiences the separation as abandonment by their parent might learn the following construct: my attachment figure could disappear at any moment and that would make me sink into harrowing feelings of emptiness, panic and abandonment. This part of the problematic model of reality is represented by a square in our Schema Map.

The existential problem also describes the worse suffering, that is, the suffering avoided by the production of the symptom, when a solution exists. In cases where no solution exists (see right-hand section of the

Schema Map), the suffering reactivates on contact with the trigger and creates an overwhelming experience; it is not contrasted with a lesser suffering.

The Solution (or Lack Thereof)

Above the roots, we find the trunk. Our tree has two trunks. The right-hand trunk, or section, represents mental models of the "helpless reactivation" type, whether or not the symptoms correspond to the official definition of post-traumatic stress disorder. This part of the model is used to define symptoms which, when triggered, produce an overwhelming emotional experience that the individual is unable to avoid. This is why there is no contrast between worse and lesser suffering in this part of the model: when a trigger in the environment activates the schema, deep suffering is immediately activated. No strategy has been put in place to avoid this suffering because no strategy is effective; that is why they are called "pro-symptom positions without a solution."

The left-hand trunk, or section, represents the larger proportion of pro-symptom constructs: pro-symptom positions that include knowledge of a solution. The urge to adapt pushes us to find strategies to escape suffering or reduce it as much as possible. When the base of the system (the existential problem and its associated suffering) is constructed, the individual is immediately driven to find a strategy to adapt to the reality they perceive. They develop this strategy with the means available to them at the stage of development they are in at the time; this is particularly important to bear in mind when working with adults. The tactic or strategy in question may be internal or behavioral and is always aimed at avoiding the suffering associated with the existential problem.

These sections above the existential problem, which contain a solution to the problem or the implicit knowledge that there is no solution (and therefore the individual is highly vulnerable and exposed) are represented by trapezoids.

The best way to maintain pro-symptom alignment or symptom coherence for the therapist is to think of these constructs as avoidance strategies and not as strategies that the individual may be using to obtain something. This helps the therapist to stay in alignment with the worse suffering, which is what makes the pro-symptom position coherent and gives meaning to the whole problematic model of reality. It is also for this reason that we refer to a passionate purpose, and that the language of the cards and open statements used in Coherence Therapy reflects the urgency to avoid the worse suffering by producing the symptom, as if the individual had no other choice, because this is indeed how the schema subjectively perceives reality.

The Situations

For a strategy to be useful, the schema needs to be able to identify the contexts in which the strategy should be deployed; this is how everyday situations are sorted by the schema. Each situation is assessed as relevant or not. The aim of this part of the system is to optimize adaptation to as many sensitive contexts as possible, thereby avoiding as much suffering as possible.

A situation will be a trigger for the schema if it represents a risk of exposing the person to a worse suffering, and therefore calls for the use of the strategy to avoid or minimize the worse suffering. This part of the model is flexible and is amended over time, through the principle of generalization. Whenever experience shows that the model is useful or relevant in a new type of situation, this situation is integrated into the problematic model of reality and the tree grows a new branch.

This explains why certain seemingly simple schemas are generalized to many contexts and seem to have taken over the entire life of the individual. Take the example of a man who has learned, on the one hand, that expressing anger cuts off all possible access to affection and compassion, and on the other, that women are deceitful and will not hesitate to betray him at the first opportunity. Here we have two mental models. The first problematic schema can only be generalized to situations in which the individual has to express his anger, while the second can easily be generalized to any situation involving a woman and will therefore be constantly activated. A situation in which this individual has to express his anger to a woman will activate both models and is likely to represent a situation that triggers a high intensity of various symptoms, since both schemas have their own adaptive solutions, like two armies rushing towards a common enemy at the same time.

The situations that trigger the schemas, which are excellent entry points for discovery work (as clarifying what they have in common enables you to quickly find your way around the model and differentiate between the different schemas), are represented by triangles in the Schema Map we have provided.

The Symptoms

Finally, let us consider the last element of our tree: the leaves. In the right-hand path, in the absence of a solution, the symptoms that make up the leaves of this tree represent the expression of the overwhelming emotion caused by the reactivation of the existential problem and its associated suffering, which is traumatic in nature and encounters no obstacle that would allow circumventing, attenuating or avoiding it. Typical examples are insomnia, anxiety, fear, helplessness (hyper-activated state) or more passive states of disconnection from certain parts of the self, such as depression, submission, and, of course, the whole range of their somatic, emotional, cognitive and behavioral expressions. Note that all of these symptoms could also be present in mental models that have a solution; they are not exclusively represented in the "no solution" map.

In the left-hand path, where the schema's astute strategist has a solution to use to avoid the worse suffering associated with the existential problem, a host of means are generally at its disposal to execute this strategy. Once again, we find the whole range of physical, kinesthetic, cognitive, emotional and behavioral symptoms in the problematic model of reality's arsenal. Few of us have experience on the battlefield, but you can imagine that wielding weapons is not done without consequences. This is how we can differentiate between so-called functional symptoms and those that have no direct function (in terms of strategy) but are rather the consequence of functional symptoms or the result of their use. Maintaining hyper-vigilance on a daily basis (strategy), notably through obsessive attention to detail (functional symptom), in order to avoid the stinging pain of humiliation (worse suffering), for example, very often leads to gastrointestinal difficulties (non-functional symptom) or initial insomnia linked to ruminations (non-functional symptom), just as engaging in perfectionist behaviors (functional symptom) can lead to chronic stress (non-functional symptom) or exhaustion (non-functional symptom).

When a symptom is a direct means of executing the strategy, or solution, it is said to be functional. However, as no strategy is perfect, its use has certain disadvantages: these resulting disadvantages are called functionless symptoms. There is no point in trying to distinguish between these symptoms at the start of exploration when the schema has not yet been fully rendered explicit. Anxiety, for example, is a highly versatile symptom that may be the manifestation of trauma reactivation, the consequence of a functional symptom, or even the functional symptom itself (in which case, activation of anxiety would be an essential part of the strategy).

The only exception to this rule concerns symptoms that aim to block all awareness of an episodic memory or the sensations which accompany the memory, that is, emotional disconnection, hyperphagia or compulsive eating, the use of alcohol or drugs (self-medication), any form of continual self-distraction via a compulsive attitude towards work or tasks or the intense excitement of video games, social media, pornography, compulsive gambling or extreme sensations, and, of course, any symptom that is obviously avoidance behavior. These symptoms can immediately be considered functional symptoms on the Schema Map.

To be in keeping with the framework of emotional coherence, all you need to do is proceed on the assumption that, whether it has a direct function or not, a symptom is always coherent within the system to which it belongs. It is perfectly normal that the therapist's empathy for the coherence of the symptom should, at the start of the therapeutic work, be at odds with the vision of clients who are opposed to their symptoms because of the suffering they cause and from which they want to be freed. In cases where the schema includes a solution to the existential problem, the client is still unaware at this point that these symptoms enable them to avoid even greater suffering.

This group of symptoms is represented by circles in the Schema Map. In the left-hand section, when a solution is foreseen by the schema, both functional and non-functional symptoms represent the lesser suffering in the system. When the system becomes fully explicit, both client and therapist are able to see that the production of functional symptoms and their consequences (non-functional symptoms) represents a necessary choice to avoid the worse suffering.

If you now imagine the tree and the associated model as an iceberg, you will be able to understand why, at the start of the work, only the leaves and a few branch tips are visible, or explicit. This part of the tree is like the tip of the iceberg and represents the field of awareness at the start of therapy. The therapist's and the client's job is to create experiences that will bring them into contact with the constructs that make up the other parts of the model, and to identify them as precisely as possible so as to be able to determine their position in the problematic model of reality and, gradually, reconstitute it as a whole so that its coherence becomes clear.

It is worth familiarizing yourself with this Schema Map when it is time to make a case presentation in supervision, for example, or when you need to take stock of the progress of your work with a given client. However, having a general working understanding of the existential problem with its specific suffering, its adaptive solution (or lack of solution), the means used to apply it (or the specific signature of the emotional state in cases where there is no solution) and the situations that trigger it, will allow you to find your bearings at all times during therapeutic work. It is a very useful way of thinking and listening during sessions and will help you stay on track and manage the heavy cognitive load that comes with working with memory reconsolidation.

Appendix 2
Mindfulness Flash Card

This card can be used when you think you recognize a reaction pattern (somatic sensations, affects, emotions, thoughts, action tendencies) linked to a schema.

Step 1

I Feel, Now, in the Present Moment

Instructions: I simply stay with what I feel in my body (somatic sensations, affects, action tendencies) for a few minutes. I observe what I am feeling without trying to change anything—If what I am feeling changes, I simply stay with the new sensation—I do not judge what is happening or cling to my thoughts; when a thought arises, I notice its presence (I can say "a thought" to myself) and return to what I am feeling. The philosophy behind this exercise is "what is, is" ("I fully realize that my schema has been reactivated").

Step 2

Why do I Have This Reaction?

Instructions: Which schema has been triggered? What is the history of this schema (hypotheses about its creation)?

Step 3

Sound Judgment

Instructions: Take the time to weigh the situation carefully. What do you feel is really true? Does another part of you feel differently, even if not totally convinced? Or does another part of you know that your schema is not totally true, even if it feels that way? Do you have any doubts, however small, about the veracity of your schema? Is your current interpretation of this situation at odds with your needs and values?

Other questions that may help: Have there been situations in the past where what you considered to be true has turned out to be false? In this particular situation, what are the facts, what are the interpretations? What would be the opinion of people close to you? Can you describe in detail the specific context of this situation? If it weren't for your fears, guilt or anger, what would you choose to do?

See your thoughts, words and images for what they are—mere thoughts, words and images—and defuse yourself from their content. Are they useful in meeting your needs and values?

Step 4

Just Action

Instructions: In this specific situation, and considering what is conceivable in reality, what I know, what is possible, as well as the means at my disposal, what is the optimal action that allows me to take into account my most fundamental needs.

Once I have identified this optimal action, I choose to do it, and I do it regardless of how I feel, and despite my propensity to flee or fight (even if I still feel my old schema).

References

Abbass, A. (2015). *Reaching through resistance: Advanced psychotherapy techniques.* Seven Leaves Press.

Arntz, A., Bernstein, D. P., & Jacob, G. (2013). *Schema therapy in practice: An introductory guide to the schema mode approach.* Wiley-Blackwell.

Arntz, A., & Van Genderen, H. (2020). *Schema therapy for borderline personality disorder* (2nd ed.). Wiley.

Barrett, L. F. (2018). *How emotions are made: The secret life of the brain.* First Mariner Books.

Beck, J. S. (2021). *Cognitive behavior therapy: Basic and beyond* (3rd ed.). Guilford Press.

Behary, W. T. (2021). *Disarming the narcissist* (3rd ed.). New Harbinger Publications.

Behary, W. T., Farrell, J. M., Vaz, A., & Rousmaniere, T. (2023). *Deliberate practice in schema therapy.* American Psychological Association.

Bennett-Goleman, T. (2001). *Emotional alchemy: How the mind can heal the heart.* Random House.

Brockman, R. N., Simpson, S., Hayes, C., van der Wijngaart, R., & Smout, M. (2023). *Cambridge guide to schema therapy.* Cambridge University Press.

Cassidy, J., & Shaver, P. R. (2016). *Handbook of attachment: Theory, research, and clinical applications* (3rd ed.). Guilford Press.

Clark, A. (2023). *The experience machine: How our minds predict and shape reality.* Pantheon Books.

Coan, J. A., & Sbarra, D. A. (2015). Social baseline theory: The social regulation of risk and effort. *Current Opinion in Psychology, 1*, 87–91. https://doi.org/10.1016/j.copsyc.2014.12.021

Coan, J. A., Schaefer, H. S., & Davidson, R. J. (2006). Lending a hand: Social regulation of the neural response to threat. *Psychological Science, 17*(12), 1032–1039.

Cooper, J. (2007). *Cognitive dissonance: Fifty years of a classic theory*. Sage Publications.

Côté, S., & Cousineau, P. (2022). *La reconsolidation thérapeutique de la mémoire: Transformer les schémas émotionnels avec la thérapie de la cohérence* [Therapeutic memory reconsolidation: Transforming emotional schemas with coherence therapy]. Dunod.

Coughlin, P. (2017). *Maximizing effectiveness in dynamic psychotherapy*. Routledge.

Cousineau, P. (2012). Mindfulness and ACT as strategies to enhance the healthy adult mode. In M. van Vreeswijk, J. Broersen, & M. Nadort (Eds.), *The Wiley-Blackwell handbook of schema therapy* (pp. 249–257). Wiley-Blackwell.

Cousineau, P., & Côté, S. (2023). *Pratiquer la thérapie des schémas: Transformer les modèles prédictifs avec la reconsolidation de la mémoire* [Practicing schema therapy: Transforming predictive models with memory reconsolidation]. Dunod.

Cousineau, P., & Ngô, T.-L. (2013). Thérapie des schémas – ACT – Pleine Conscience (Schema Therapy – ACT – Mindfulness). *Santé mentale au Québec, 38*(2), 195–213. https://doi.org/10.7202/1023996ar

Damasio, A. (1999). *The feeling of what happens: Body and emotion in the making of consciousness*. Harcourt Brace & Co.

Damasio, A. (2021). *Feeling and knowing: Making mind conscious*. Pantheon Books.

Ecker, B. (2018). Clinical translation of memory reconsolidation research: Therapeutic methodology for transformational change by erasing implicit emotional learnings driving symptom production. *International Journal of Neuropsychotherapy, 6*(1), 1–92.

Ecker, B., & Hulley, L. (1996). *Depth oriented brief therapy: How to be brief when you were trained to be deep – and vice versa*. Jossey-Bass.

Ecker, B., & Hulley, L. (2019). *Coherence therapy practice manual and training guide*. Coherence Psychology Institute. www.coherencetherapy.org/resources/manual.htm

Ecker, B., Ticic, R., & Hulley, L. (2012). *Unlocking the emotional brain: Eliminating symptoms at their roots using memory reconsolidation*. Routledge.

Ecker, B., Ticic, R., & Hulley, L. (2024). *Unlocking the emotional brain: Memory reconsolidation and the psychotherapy of transformational change* (2nd ed.). Routledge.

Ecker, B., Vaz, A. (2022). Memory reconsolidation and the crisis of mechanism in psychotherapy. *New Ideas in Psychology, 66*, 1–11. https://psycnet.apa.org/doi/10.1016/j.newideapsych.2022.100945

Edelman, G. (1989). *The remembered present: A biological theory of consciousness*. Basic Books.

Edwards, D. J. A. (2022). Using schema modes for case conceptualization in schema therapy: An applied clinical approach. *Frontiers in Psychology, 12*, Article 819206. https://doi.org/10.3389/fpsyg.2021.763670

Farrell, J. M., Reiss, N., & Shaw, I. A. (2014). *The schema therapy clinician's guide: A complete resource for building and delivering individual, group and integrated schema mode treatment programs*. Wiley Blackwell.

Farrell, J. M., & Shaw, I. A. (2012). *Group schema therapy for borderline personality disorder: A step-by-step treatment manual with patient workbook*. Wiley-Blackwell.

Fonagy, P., Gergely, G., Jurist, E., & Target, M. (2002). *Affect regulation, mentalization, and the development of the self*. Other Press.

Fosha, D. (2021). *Undoing aloneness & the transformation of suffering into flourishing: AEDP 2.0*. American Psychological Association.

Frederickson, J. (2021). *Co-creating safety: Healing the fragile patient*. Seven Leaves Press.

Grawe, K. (2007). *Neuropsychotherapy: How the neurosciences inform effective psychotherapy*. Psychology Press.

Harris, R. (2007). *The happiness trap: Stop struggling, start living*. Exisle Publishing.

Hayes, S. C., Strosahl, K. D., & Wilson, K. G. (1999). *Acceptance and commitment therapy: An experiential approach to behavior change*. Guilford Press.

Hayes, S. C., Strosahl, K. D., & Wilson, K. G. (2012). *Acceptance and commitment therapy: The process and practice of mindful change* (2nd ed.). Guilford Press.

Hebb, D. O. (2009). *The organization of behavior*. Taylor & Francis (Original work published 1949).

Hohwy, J. (2013). *The predictive mind*. Oxford University Press.

Jacob, G., & Arntz, A. (2021). *La thérapie des schémas en pratique: Principes et outils* [Schema therapy in practice: Principles and tools] (J.-M. Fichel, Trans.). De Boeck (Original work published 2015).

Jeffers, S. (2007). *Feel the fear... and do it anyway*. Jeffers Press.

Leng, G. (2018). *The heart of the brain: The hypothalamus and its hormones*. The MIT Press.

Levine, P. A. (1997). *Waking the tiger – Healing trauma*. North Atlantic Books.

Levine, P. A. (2010). *In an unspoken voice: How the body releases trauma and restores goodness*. North Atlantic Books.

Lewis, M. (2015). *The biology of desire: Why addiction is not a disease*. Doubleday Canada.

Loose, C., Graaf, P., Zarbock, G., & Holt, R. A. (2020). *Schema therapy for children and adolescents: A practitioner's guide*. Pavilion Publishing and Media.

McGilchrist, I. (2009). *The master and his emissary: The divided brain and the making of the western world*. Yale University Press.

McGilchrist, I. (2021). *The matter with things: Our brains, our delusions, and the unmaking of the world.* Perspective Press.

Mercier, H., & Sperber, D. (2017). *The enigma of reason.* Harvard University Press.

Miller, A. (2008). *The drama of the gifted child: The search for the true self.* Basic Books (Original work published 1979).

Panksepp, J. (1998). *Affective neuroscience: The foundations of human and animal emotions.* Oxford University Press.

Panksepp, J., & Biven L. (2012). *The archeology of mind: Neuroevolutionary origins of human emotions.* W. W. Norton.

Proust, M. (1992). *In search of lost time: The complete masterpiece* (C. K. Scott Moncrief, T. Kilmartin, & A. Mayor, Trans.). The Modern Library (Original work published 1913–1927).

Proust, M. (2023). *Swann's way* (J. Grieve, Trans.). New York Review of Books (Original work published 1913).

Roediger, E., Stevens, B. A., & Brockman, R. (2018). *Contextual schema therapy: An integrative approach to personality disorders, emotional dysregulation & interpersonal functioning.* Context Press.

Ryan, R. M., & Deci, E. L. (2017). *Self-determination theory: Basic psychological needs in motivation, development, and wellness.* Guilford Press.

Sapolsky, R. M. (2023). *Determined: A science of life without free will.* Penguin Press.

Seth, A. (2021). *Being you: A new science of consciousness.* Dutton.

Siegel, D. J. (2012). *Pocket guide to interpersonal neurobiology: An integrative handbook of the mind.* W. W. Norton.

Siegel, D. J. (2020). *The developing mind: How relationships and the brain interact to shape who you are* (3rd ed.). Guilford Press.

Simpson, S. (2020). Schema therapy assessment of eating disorders. In S. Simpson, & E. Smith (Eds.), *Schema therapy for eating disorders: Theory and practice for individual and group settings* (pp. 37–55). Routledge.

Smucker, M. R., Dancu, V. C., Foa, E. B., & Niederee, L. J. (1995). Imagery rescripting: A new treatment for survivors of childhood sexual abuse suffering from posttraumatic stress. *Journal of Cognitive Psychotherapy, 9*(1), 3–17.

Solms, M. (2015). *The feeling brain: Selected papers on neuropsychoanalysis.* Karnac Books.

Solms, M. (2021). *The hidden spring: A journey to the source of consciousness.* W. W. Norton.

Stark, M. (2017). *Relentless hope: The refusal to grieve.* e-Book International Psychotherapy Institute. www.freepsychotherapybooks.org/ebook/relentless-hope-2/

Tulving, E. (1972). Episodic and semantic memory. In E. Tulving, & W. Donaldson (Eds.), *Organization of memory* (pp. 381–402). Academic Press.

van der Wijngaart, R. (2021). *Imagery rescripting: Theory and practice*. Pavilion Publishing and Media.

Wegner, D. M. (2002). *The illusion of conscious will*. MIT Press.

Wilson, E. O. (2015). *The meaning of human existence*. Liveright Publishing.

Winnicott, D. W. (2005). *Playing and reality*. Routledge (Original work published 1971).

Young, J. E. (1990). *Cognitive therapy for personality disorders: A schema-focused approach*. Professional Resource Exchange.

Young, J. E., Klosko, J. S., & Weishaar, M. E. (2003). *Schema therapy: A practitioner's guide*. The Guilford Press.

Index

www.ingramcontent.com/pod-product-compliance
Ingram Content Group UK Ltd.
Pitfield, Milton Keynes, MK11 3LW, UK
UKHW022355190926
475702UK00015B/2301

* 9 7 8 1 0 4 1 0 4 3 7 8 2 *